Developing a
Successful Elementary School
Media Center

LILLIAN GLOGAU

EDMUND KRAUSE

MIRIAM WEXLER

PARKER PUBLISHING COMPANY, INC.   WEST NYACK, N.Y.

© 1972 by

PARKER PUBLISHING COMPANY, INC.

West Nyack, N.Y.

Library of Congress
Catalog Card Number: 74-164897

Printed in the United States of America
ISBN-0-13-205096-X
B & P

Developing
a Successful
Elementary School
Media Center

PREVIOUS BOOKS BY THE AUTHORS

THE NONGRADED PRIMARY SCHOOL: A CASE STUDY
Glogau and Fessel (Parker)
YOU AND NEW YORK CITY
Glogau and Krause (Benefic)
LET'S SEE
Glogau and Krause (American Optometric Assn.)

The Practical Value of
a Media Center

This is a practical book intended to help educators start or expand media centers. Everything we describe or discuss has been or is being done in our own schools. We know media centers work. Few educators are against media centers. Most of them feel, however, that their schools, as presently constructed, cannot house a media center. Others feel that the expenses involved are too high. We wish to belie both these fears.

Many elementary school plants have woefully inadequate facilities for developing media centers. It is our hope that we can show educators that the most humble elementary school facilities can be rearranged, reorganized, or restructured to encompass the media center concept. Adaptability is the key word. Adaptability and commitment to the need for a media center. Proper planning to insure a media center, even one of modest proportions, can take place once the commitment is made and without undue expense.

This book is planned as a down-to-earth guide for incorporating a media center into any school. We deal with such complexities as the quality and quantity of soft and hardware necessary to launch a media center. We endeavor to show how the materials of the media center can be planned to correlate with the school's ongoing curriculum; and how, in large measure, the center can be made to expand the school's curriculum into more rarefied areas such as love of reading, appreciation of film, listening to sounds, and love of pictorial beauty. We try to show ways and means of winning over the most reluctant faculty to the real use of a media center. We explore the dual leadership roles of the librarian and administrator and their relationships necessary in establishing a working media center. On a very practical level types and kinds of elementary school library schedules are examined. Those which are constituted to enhance a media center's effectiveness in the total school programs are described.

Many schools have part-time librarians, some have full-time librarians, some have none. We have included enough concrete units of study for a librarian's use to enable the most inexperienced librarian to become a cracker-jack media specialist. There are many specific activities, games and puzzles which teachers and the librarian can use most effectively with their children. Each activity developed is designed to reinforce a minimum of one media center goal or library skill. We carefully delineate the four basic goals of an effective media program and you will find that all these goals have specific primary and intermediate projects described for their proper development with children.

Audio-visual hard and software are discussed at length. The role of each machine and examples of its use as it relates to some curriculum goal are explained. We have included, too, some creative experiences with audio-visual equipment which can enhance any school's program.

The American Library Association standards for media centers are included, though we feel they represent the ultimate and schools should work toward these standards over a period of time. We know from our own experiences that one can incorporate modified plans for media centers with much success. We certainly hope to reach the standards in the years to come. In the meantime, we take small steps forward and these small steps have rewarded our school, our program and our children immeasurably.

In order to stem the tide of negative reactions, such as "Our library is too small for a media center" or "We don't have enough money to equip a media center" we have included precise methods and techniques for launching media centers with limited capital and space. What is required, as we have previously stated, is commitment to the media center concept. After that, one can take steps to begin building a media center in any school. Floor plans will show how ordinary classrooms have been converted into media centers with a little imagination. Plans for media centers without elaborate expenditures are possible.

Certain strategies are needed to build media centers and to incorporate the media center program into an ongoing school's operational pattern. First, there must be commitment to the idea itself. This commitment must come first and foremost from the principal. It is he who will guide the program, build it, encourage it. Second, teachers must be committed to the media-center concept. Here the principal must use his ingenuity and leadership to inspire teachers with the media center concept. Third, is the librarian himself. He must be of special mettle. If he is a gifted librarian, he will do most of the selling of the concept himself, but he will also serve as director and guide through the intricacies of planning the new undertaking. Fourth, one needs to plan for the ordering of materials, hard and soft, which fulfill the needs of the school's curriculum, as well as fulfilling the goals of the media center program. Fifth, one needs some workable space in the school building where this material can be stored. A central place is ideal, but not necessary. Sixth, schedules for the effective operation of the media center must be developed. Seventh, specific techniques for translating all phases of the media center's program directly into the children's learning experiences must be developed.

These strategies for the development of a media center may indeed sound complex. We must assure you from experience that they can be accomplished, in large measure, with good planning and cooperation among key members of the school staff, namely, the principal and the librarian. The important thing is to start. One can start on a very small scale with very simple plans. But start one must, before schools become so dull for our children that they will in the vernacular "turn us off" completely.

Our book should help educators go through the seven steps to a media center. This is our intent in writing the book. For example, the chapters on the development of skills activities for children on all instructional levels with precise examples of each skill, can be lifted in toto by the pressured librarian busy with the intricacies of ordering and setting up shop, for use just as they are. In the more peaceful years to come the librarian will wish to develop his own lessons and activities, but there is no harm in using short cuts like these in the first year or two of operation. In fact, administrators and librarians alike would be wise to borrow many ideas presented throughout this book without bothering to develop new, complex ones of their own during the start of their own programs when they are so rushed for time.

We are presenting a practical thesis which can actually be used by schools to help them launch their own media centers, if they have not already done so. The authors can no longer imagine a school in existence today without such a center and would feel proud if they help serve as a conversion source.

Lillian Glogau
Edmund Krause
Miriam Wexler

Contents

The Media Center Is an Environment
Creating the Environment
How Much Is Enough?
The Media Program Depends on Your Educational Objectives
Identify Your Priorities
Developing a Media Program for a Hypothetical School
Where It's At; or the Status Quo
Preparations for a Classroom-Centered Media Program
Phasing the Pilot Plan
Budget for Phase I
Phase I: The Media Program in the Classroom
Phase II: Planning the Media Center While Continuing
  the Media Program in the Classroom

Children Become Authors
For Remedial Purposes and Individualization
Enrichment Through Myths
Enrichment Through Folklore
Enrichment Through Nursery Rhymes
Music Correlation
Film Production

The 16mm Projector
Overhead Projector
Tape Recorder
Filmstrip and/or Slide Projector
Media Center Aides and Other Teacher Helpers

Shortcomings of the Present School Library
Inexpensive Arrangements for a One-Room Media Center Core from Your Present Library
Summary and Some Cost Estimates for One-Room Media Centers
Some Inexpensive Ideas Where There Is Little Room for Storage
Redesign Using an Adjacent Room
Redesign Using an Entire Floor
A Novel Plan for Redesigning a Media Center for a Two-Story School

Modern Public Library as Heart of New School
Open Space Precedent in One-Room Schoolhouse
Self-Contained Classroom Antecedents
Design Schools for Children and Flexibility
Highlights of Schools Using Media

Problems in Designing and Building New Schools
Ideas to Consider for Media-Designed Schools

Developing
a Successful
Elementary School
Media Center

1

Planning and Ordering
for a Media Center

What are Media Centers made of?

Of kids who are wired,
Who never get tired
Of listening and looking
To see what is cooking!

THE MEDIA CENTER IS AN ENVIRONMENT

As in a kitchen where good cooking is in progress and delicious smells entice to lift the lids of the pots to see what is cooking, the media center should always have many pots boiling. It should provide an environment that motivates to taste and also to want to do some cooking of your own. It should invite to browse, and to discover, with its many centers of interest and displays. Its workaday operating procedures should be so simple that children from the age of 7 on up can handle all of them with very little help and only occasional supervision. Ideally it should be able to advertise its wares, following the boutique idea of sophisticated stores. That's why it needs to be arranged as flexibly as possible, so that even the location of the displays can be varied to attract the eye to areas never before discovered.

CREATING THE ENVIRONMENT

To create a media environment you need:

A listening area with open access to recordings and/or tape and record players and tape recorders on tables nearby, plugged in and ready to go.

A viewing area, furnished with various kinds of viewing equipment such as filmstrip previewers, filmloop projectors, and sound filmstrips previewers in carrels and easy access to filmstrip loops and sound filmstrip sets.

A story and quiet reading area with either comfortable furniture, an area rug, pillows, hassocks, or carpeted deep steps or a combination of any or all of these.

A reference and study area near the reference materials and card catalog.

A discussion area for small groups.

A display area in which children's contributions, related to a given subject can be displayed, such as an egg tree with hand-decorated easter eggs in the spring, a listening post with poetry created by children on tape, or a display of origami and other handcrafts done by children coordinated with related craft books.

A circulation area so arranged that the children can handle their transactions independently.

A circulation, storage and repair area for those pieces of A-V equipment which are not permanently stationed in the classroom, off the media center, so that their circulation does not interfere with the traffic in the center.

A media specialist who can create such environment, who has a library degree with a specialization in children's services, who is creative, has a lot of energy and can work in a noisy, busy environment, who knows children and children's books intimately and is equally conversant with the other media in the center, who is able to organize all media for easy accessibility to all and knows how to relate them to the curriculum, and last but not least, is not afraid of a screwdriver, so that he can make small repairs on the spot.

Enough equipment and materials, (software), books and periodicals to service your school regardless of its organization.

HOW MUCH IS ENOUGH?

Let's begin here: with the equipment, software and books. What is enough? Fortunately for schools that wish to begin a media program, there now exist new standards. In 1969 the National Education Association (NEA), jointly with the American Library Association (ALA), published *Standards for School Media Programs*. Although these SSMP are in part quantitative, based on student enrollment figures, their most important aim is:

> ... to present standards for media programs that will best aid the schools in implementing their educational goals and instructional programs. The standards are designed for schools seeking to give young people education of good quality. Schools with innovative curricula and instructional techniques will need and want to go beyond the quantitative standards, *but for schools which have not yet fully achieved their objectives, the standards can serve as a guide for charting goals to be reached in progressive steps over a planned period of time.* [1]   (italics added)

These standards are extremely useful, especially because they are not rigid and allow for the kind of program-oriented budgeting system which is presently gaining ground in many school systems in the United States.[2]

THE MEDIA PROGRAM DEPENDS ON YOUR EDUCATIONAL OBJECTIVES

Therefore the question "What is enough?" depends on your educational objectives. A media program must provide support and services for the instructional program in language arts, social studies, science, music, health and art, and also must motivate each student to become an independent learner. What are your educational objectives? It will be easier to isolate them by examining some of the salient features of your educational program. Ask yourself the following questions:

> Do you use a multi-text approach in science and social studies?
> In reading do you use basal and supplementary texts? Tradebooks?
> Do you allow children to progress at their own rate in math?
> Do you teach by the problem solving method in science and social studies?

---

1. American Association of School Librarians and the Department of Audiovisual Instruction of the National Education Association. *Standards for School Media Programs,* ALA and NEA 1969.

2. Barry Morris, in "Budgeting to Meet the New Standards," *School Activities and the Library,* ALA 1970, p.5, discusses the Planning Programming Budgeting System (PPBS) as it affects the school media budget.

Do you teach research skills in the classroom?

Are teachers allowed some experimentation in the classroom?

Do you participate in some form of team teaching or regrouping?

Do your students work in groups or committees?

Do you teach by the unit method?

Do students in your class teach each other?

Do your students produce learning materials to present what they have learned?

Are individual students permitted to pursue something that interests them alone?

Do you try to individualize your instruction?

Do you have a core curriculum?

Are your assembly programs the result of work in the classroom?

If you can answer yes to even one of these questions, a media center will help to fulfill these goals. From the answers to these questions you can formulate your present educational objectives and those you wish to add. From these objectives you can then develop a long-range plan for a media center program with the new *Standards for School Media Programs* as a guide. Utopian as they may seem for those schools which are beginning from absolute scratch and are even without a central library facility, they can easily be adapted to any situation, stated in terms of educational objectives to be achieved. All you need do when your educational objectives are clearly defined is identify your priorities and phase them according to available funds over a predetermined span of time.

IDENTIFY YOUR PRIORITIES

Your priorities will in great part depend on the organizational patterns of your school, the socio-economic background of your school community, your community resources, the teaching styles of your staff and your curricular structure, combined with the quantitative factor of your student enrollment. In other words: your instructional program which is a function of all these factors is more important in developing your media program than your enrollment figure.

Whatever your situation is, begin "where you are at," always keeping in mind the interrelationship of all media and prorating your funds to achieve a balance between all media, as recommended in the *Standards for School Media Programs.*[3]

DEVELOPING A MEDIA PROGRAM FOR A HYPOTHETICAL SCHOOL

Allowing for some variations all schools can be classified as either:

classroom centered,	schools where most instruction and learning takes place in the self-contained classroom, and which have no central library.
library centered,	schools with self-contained classrooms and a central library.
media centered,	schools built wholly or in part to facilitate grouping and regrouping of students for instruction, independent study, and production of media.

WHERE IT'S AT; OR THE STATUS QUO

Let's take a look at a hypothetical elementary school built 30 years ago. There are many schools like this in use today all over the U.S. Chestnut School is a classroom-centered school, because it was built when libraries were hardly ever included in elementary schools. At present it has five classrooms on every grade level and two kindergarten rooms. It does have in every classroom a small collection of curriculum-centered, nonfiction and fiction trade books for pleasure reading. Each teacher has a yearly allotment of $50.00 towards this classroom library. Each grade level has over the years accumulated a considerable number of duplicate copies, simply because teachers mostly used the same sources to purchase from, namely the bibliographies in their textbooks—"for further reading." The quality of the collections is not outstanding, mainly because many textbook publishers list books in the sale of which they have a residual interest. The average number of books in each classroom does not run over 50, because outdated and worn books need to be replaced and $50.00 does not go very far today. Books are rarely shared among the classes on the same grade level, first because there are many duplications and secondly a proprietary attitude by teachers towards their books persists.

---

3. ALA and Dept. of A-V Instructions of N.E.A., *Standards for School Media Programs,* ALA, and NEA 1969, pp. 35,36.

Housed in a room off the principal's office, Chestnut has a small filmstrip collection of about 300 titles covering most subject areas, but not equally well. Here too, is a collection of about 50 recordings, many of them in poor condition, and a sign-out book to show who took what, and when. Most of the time the materials you are looking for are not there and when you start sleuthing around for them, you find out that the person who signed for them last is not the same person who has them now. You have to follow the trail to the last user and unless you are very persistent, you give up and do without. Even had you found them, it would be a neat trick to pry one of the few working filmstrip projectors loose from someone, who seems to think that he has a monopoly on it, because he fixed it once. Does this sound familiar?

PREPARATIONS FOR A CLASSROOM-CENTERED MEDIA PROGRAM

Take heart! All this will soon be a nightmare of the past. Because of pressure of the staff under the principal's leadership, the district has allowed Chestnut School to develop a pilot plan for a media program, ultimately resulting in a media-centered school. Enough money has been found to hire a media specialist and a half-time media aide[4] for the remainder of the current school year (4 months).

A media specialist answering to the description above is found. The room off the principal's office becomes his headquarters. He takes an inventory of all existing equipment and A-V media and organizes them for circulation. He repairs what he can and arranges for outside repair services for more seriously damaged equipment. The media aide types pockets and cards for all pieces of equipment and recordings which are not discarded, as well as circulation cards for the filmstrips which are still current and serviceable. An inventory card is prepared for each item retained. From the information on this inventory card, catalog card sets are typed at a later date. (For the filmstrips the circulation card serves as the inventory card.) Until the catalog cards are typed for the existing A-V media, a subject list of filmstrips and recordings is typed and distributed to all teachers. The classroom book collections are inventoried next, without ever leaving the classroom. Only out-of-date materials are discarded. Out of the total collection of 1500, 1000 volumes are retained, including up to four copies of useful titles.

4. *Op. cit.* p. xv.

PHASING THE PILOT PLAN

With the help of the media specialist the planning moves into high gear. Because the financial situation of the school district is favorable, it is decided to phase in a media program over a period of three years. (Of course if this proves to be too much of a financial burden, a four- or five-year plan could be worked out, but if at all possible, decide to see it through in three years, lest it lose the interest of the faculty.) For best and most tangible results each phase of the plan will have as its aim the accomplishment of specific educational objectives spelled out in detail. The objectives for phase 1 of the media program at Chestnut School are:

   a. Strong emphasis on the problem-solving approach in teaching, to develop independent thinking. (In the science area)
   b. Individualization through a greater variety of diverse resources on many levels.
   c. A program of operational skills of various A-V equipment for students and teachers.

To implement these three objectives it will be necessary at first to establish a classroom-based media program. The media specialist suggests that it would be advisable to concentrate all purchases of nonprint materials in one subject area only. Why? Results will appear faster this way than by proliferating the resources in many subject areas. When results become visible, enthusiasm for the media program will grow apace.

The district has just published a new science curriculum K-12. Some of the faculty at Chestnut were involved in the writing of it. Here is a good starting point for the ordering of a science media collection and, at the same time, bringing the new curriculum to the attention of the total staff. The media specialist furnishes each grade level committee with selection tools and quality catalogs so that its members can expand the biblographies already in the curriculum for ordering this same year. The principal and media specialist decide that initially each grade level will order the filmstrip, filmloop, recording tape, and transparency listings suggested in the new science curriculum plus additional titles of each of these media to achieve a total complement of 500 filmstrip and 100 filmloop titles as well as 100 recordings and/or tapes, not including the media which were part of the inventory just completed. These figures were arrived at by dividing by three the basic quantitative standards as suggested in the

Standards for School Media Programs for these particular media.[5] To utilize the newly ordered resources each classroom will be provided with a hanging screen, a filmstrip projector and a record player. A tape recorder will be purchased for every three classrooms, an overhead projector for every five. The small amount of equipment presently owned by the school will be used as reserve equipment. The media specialist will order enough books (preprocessed) so that at the beginning of the next school year the total book collection will be 3000 volumes strong.

BUDGET FOR PHASE I

The equipment and resources below, when purchased, will be distributed to classrooms.   *Items will be housed in the media headquarters and will circulate upon request.   **Items remain in media headquarters and are used there.

EQUIPMENT

```
 ** 1  thermal copier (transparency maker)
    30  hanging screens (70x70) with keystone eliminator
    30  record players
    30  filmstrip projectors
    10  tape recorders with microphones
     6  portable overhead projectors
  * 3  filmloop projectors (super 8)
  * 2  autoload 16 mm projectors
  * 1  opaque projector for each floor of the school
     3  projection carts (1 for each piece of non-portable equip-
        ment)
   120  padded earphones
    30  input boxes
```

RESOURCES

```
  2000  books, preprocessed and with printed catalog card sets
  *  500  filmstrips (science) including sound filmstrip sets
  *  100  filmloops (science) super 8
  *  200  recordings and/or tapes (science)
  *   12  prepared transparency sets
          films (16 mm)[6]
```

---

5. *Op. cit.* p. 30.

6. In this district films are purchased centrally and are distributed upon request by an interschool courier service.

SUPPLIES A-V

** Transparency supplies for the thermal copier
     transparency sheets (clear acetate)
     pens for overhead projectors
 * recording tape and take-up reels
** spirit masters for thermal copier
** replacement bulbs for all projectors
 * extra take-up reels for 16mm projector

SUPPLIES LIBRARY

** the usual library supplies
** catalog card kits for existing collection of books
     (printed)[7]
** color-coded catalog cards for the cataloging of various
     nonprint media

OFFICE EQUIPMENT AND FURNITURE

** 1 typewriter
** 1 secretary's desk and chair
** 1 15-drawer card catalog cabinet
** 1 4-drawer shelflist cabinet
** 2 2-drawer steel filing cabinets to blend with the card
     catalog cabinet.

The work of the media specialist during this time will be confined to the ordering, processing and cataloging of all materials. He becomes acquainted with the curriculum by meeting with teachers at grade level meetings and by studying curriculum guides and texts used.

The media aide does all the clerical work and filing necessary for ordering and processing materials as they come in. Constructing a card catalog, under the supervision of the media specialist, and maintaining an accurate circulation system is another of her responsibilities. The media specialist and aide work during the summer, so that when school opens in September of the next school year, most of the materials that have arrived are ready and cataloged.

---

7. Pockets and book cards are pasted in when they arrive to facilitate circulation and control by the classroom teacher.

PHASE I: THE MEDIA PROGRAM IN THE CLASSROOM

Assuming that all equipment has arrived before the opening of school, every classroom has now been outfitted with a screen, a record player, a filmstrip projector, an input box and 4 earphones. Except for the screens these pieces of equipment are signed out to the classroom teacher. The equipment is distributed as previously indicated and charged to a teacher who assumes responsibility for sharing it with a group of three or five others. The 16mm projectors and opaque projector are housed in the media specialist's office (the room adjacent to the principal's office where equipment formerly was stored) and are borrowed on a reservation basis. Films ordered from the district for teachers are listed weekly so that they may be utilized fully by all who wish to take advantage of them.

During Phase I, the work of the media specialist is apportioned between organizational and teaching duties. He prepares cross-media bibliographies even before the materials arrive, relating print and nonprint materials to the curriculum. This is particularly important at this time because the cross-media card catalog never quite keeps pace with the incoming materials, and getting all the media that are pertinent to teachers' programs in their hands fast and frequently is the key to a successful media program.

Even with preprocessed books and printed catalog card sets for A-V materials, whenever they are available—and at this writing they are not yet available for all materials in a uniform *simple* format—it takes time to scan all card sets for additional subject headings, where the printed heading is too scholarly for elementary schools, and make "see" references. Cross references are made later, when the card catalog is at least 75% complete. The media specialist continues to attend grade level meetings. Here he finds out what teachers need most in the way of materials. He sees to it that the collections in their classrooms reflect the work that is current there, and teachers cooperate by staggering their units to be able to take optimum advantage of the available resources. At grade level meetings and in the classrooms the media specialist discovers the teaching styles and approaches of many staff members to the curriculum, which helps him to suggest interesting and novel ways of using the new hardware. In the classroom the media specialist works with large and small groups of children to teach them how to operate and care for the new equipment. The media specialist with interested teachers and/or the principal organizes a number of workshops in which all teachers learn the simple mechanics needed to keep their equipment operational, and also some of the new teaching techniques available to them because of it. Concurrently the media specialist, with a small committee of teachers representing primary and intermediate areas, is involved in detailed planning of the media center conversion or addition which is to be begun in Phase II.

PHASE II: PLANNING THE MEDIA CENTER WHILE CONTINUING THE MEDIA PROGRAM IN THE CLASSROOM

It is decided that next year's emphasis will be in the social studies area and the budget for Phase II is drawn up as follows:

EQUIPMENT

** 1 thermal book copier
    5 tape recorders and microphones
    3 portable overhead projectors
    3 filmloop projectors (super 8)
 * 1 slide carrousel
   15 filmstrip previewers

RESOURCES

 * 2000 books, preprocessed and with printed catalog card sets
 * 500 filmstrips (social studies) including sound filmstrip sets
 * 100 loop films, super 8, (social studies)
 *   12 prepared transparency sets (social studies)
 * 500 slides (art, social studies)

SUPPLIES A-V

See: Phase I supplies for new equipment, including blank filmstrip footage

SUPPLIES LIBRARY

See: Phase I

OFFICE EQUIPMENT AND FURNITURE

 * 1 typewriter
** 1 15-drawer card catalog

** 1 2-drawer addition to shelflist cabinet
** 2 2-drawer steel files (as before)

The educational objectives of Phase II of the media program are:

a. Applying the problem-solving approach in teaching to the social studies area.
b. Emphasis on small-group team work in reporting by children.
c. Teaching children how to produce media for the presentation of their work.

To help teachers accomplish the first goal the media specialist develops an in-service course in which each teacher adapts one of his units in social studies to the discovery method, and appends a bibliography of pertinent media, or writes an original unit in this fashion.

At grade level meetings the media specialist develops standards with the teachers on each level by which to judge team reports by children, with emphasis on comparison of available media and production techniques.

In the classroom the media specialist teaches how to compare sources and how to produce simple media for reporting purposes.

Administratively, the media specialist orders furniture and equipment which will be used solely in the media center, over and above the equipment already in use in the classrooms. Whatever physical plan for the media center has been developed, it will have to provide for:

1. a minimum seating area for 30-40 students or 1/20 of your total enrollment.
2. a wet (wired) carrel area which can seat at least 20 more children.
3. a viewing or listening area nearby for 2 small groups (6-8), preferably at round tables, most economic of space.
4. a story and fiction-browsing area (a good place in rear of the carrel area because of the barrier formed by carrels).
5. a circulation of materials area.
6. a reference and card catalog area.
7. a production area, separate, but visible through a glass partition with a dark room and soundproof area for taping.
8. an office and processing area with enough open shelving for materials waiting to be processed and storage space for supplies.

9. a teacher preparation area with a typewriter and storage for periodical backfiles, professional library, samples of supplementary texts, a counter for a ditto machine and thermal copier(s). In new buildings best use of space is made if the media center is on the ground floor, accessible directly from the outside and close to administrative offices and faculty room for common use of duplicating equipment.

10. some wall display space in all of the above areas with generous display space on walls and shelf tops in the story area.

11. an A-V equipment storage, repair and circulation area for equipment not on permanent loan to the classrooms.

12. a conference room where small groups can discuss their projects.

13. a large group instruction area with projection equipment, a teaching wall (if so desired), light control panel, television set.

14. carpeting throughout except in the production area.

Before he decides what type of furniture to buy, he considers these rules of thumb: the more flexible the furniture the better, permitting environmental change when needed. He investigates shelving on rolling casters or slides. Under no circumstances does he want to have it built in. That is a way for architects to make money on subcontractors and for subcontractors to stick you with shoddy workmanship because of low bids. He considers making provisions for shelving all media on one subject together. Many library furniture and supply companies now manufacture shelving for filmstrips and recordings, tapes and loops in small sections which can be put on the same shelves as the printed materials. If classified according to the Dewey Decimal System, all A-V materials can be shelved following the printed materials at the end of each 100. When shelved together, children and teachers perceive the media as related, no matter what their format. To accomplish this togetherness, he discovers that shelves must be at least 10 inches deep to accommodate recordings and sound filmstrip sets.

The media specialist is now about to draw up his furniture order. He remembers that he already has:

a 30-drawer card catalog
a 6-drawer shelflist catalog
1 secretary desk and chair

   2 typewriters
   4 2-drawer steel filing cabinets in the desired color

He orders: FURNITURE

carpeting to be installed wall to wall
shelving to house up to 8000 books, doublefaced, freestanding
    on rollers or sliding casters; low, 4-5ft. for fiction collection
   6 ft. for nonfiction collection, minimum 10" deep shelving for
     filmstrips
   4 regular book trucks, wood
   2 small book trucks with slanting shelves
   2 swivel secretary chairs
   1 circulation desk
   4 stepping stools
  10 sitting stools or firm pillows for story area
   2 desk lamps for desks in office area (if inside room)
  20 wet carrels, desk surface no higher than 26 inches
  60 chairs
   2 round tables
   4 rectangular tables (5 x 3')
   1 map storage case for posters, etc.

EQUIPMENT (previously purchased)

He leaves: 1 record player, 1 filmstrip projector and 4 headphones
and 1 input box in each classroom permanently signed out to each
teacher for the school year. He parks all equipment which was
previously shared by more than 1 classroom teacher in the A-V
storage area to be circulated whenever needed. All equipment has
pockets and cards affixed with serial number marked and is identified as property of Chestnut School. The type of bulb used in each
piece of equipment is marked on the pocket for speedy replacement.

He orders: EQUIPMENT (for use in the media center only)

   1 autoload 16mm projector
   4 super 8mm filmloop projectors
   3 cassette tape recorders
   2 record players
   1 super 8 sound film projector
  10 filmstrip previewers (6x6" screen min.)
   5 instamatic cartridge load cameras
  12 padded earphones of high quality

 4 input boxes
 1 polaroid camera

RESOURCES

2000 books, preprocessed and with printed catalog cards
 500 filmstrips concentrated in areas not previously covered,
      including sound filmstrip sets
 100 filmloops
40-50 periodical subscriptions, including professional

SUPPLIES A-V

same as before depending on inventory on hand, plus film for
cameras and take-up reels for 8mm film projector

SUPPLIES LIBRARY

Same as before depending on inventory on hand plus princeton
files for backfiling of periodicals and periodical record cards

PHASE III: COMPLETION OF MEDIA CENTER

During Phase III the media center is completed. As soon as the
workmen have moved out, the media specialist moves his office in.
The book collections in the classrooms are now moved to the media
center. So are all other media and all equipment (hardware) which
must be shared by more than one classroom teacher (single-starred
items on the equipment list). The information (vertical) files are
moved in and, most important, the media card catalog in which all
media are cataloged on color-coded cards, rendering the previously
made media lists obsolete.

Throughout this chapter we have dealt with a physical plant in
which no central library existed, which is why a collection of up to
5000 volumes was distributed to classrooms to be circulated from
there, under the teacher's supervision. In a library-centered school
with only enough space for traditional library equipment and printed
materials, during the conversion period the media specialist uses the
library room as a base of operations. Everything else remains the
same as in the classroom-centered situation until the media center is
completed. It is possible but extremely difficult and cumbersome to
administer a conventional library program and concurrently develop
a media program. It is better and simpler to distribute the existing
print collection (books) in classrooms, according to reading level and

curriculum needs, to avoid the time-consuming tasks of circulation by and for individuals.

PHASE III: EDUCATIONAL OBJECTIVES

The educational objectives of Phase III are the teaching of library research and reference skills, utilizing all media, and a literature program supported by print and nonprint materials which originates from the media specialist.

The new media center is always open to everyone because of the imaginative and skillful balancing of time blocks for specific educational goals, so that everyone gets an opportunity to come, individually, in small or large groups when the media specialist is available for them. Now that the media center is open for business, what might one expect to see there in the span of an hour's time?

Here is a kaleidoscopic view of an actual media center in operation at the Elmwood School, Monsey, N.Y.:

Children from all levels are in the center at the same time. Seven-year-old Scott and Adele are each threading a filmstrip in a previewer. Each is doing a report on a different animal. They have just chosen a few filmstrips on their topic from the filmstrip cabinets (close to the circulation desk and the carrel area) to which they have browsing access. They apparently found their strips without help, but Adele comes over tò say that she had to help Scott with his filmstrip because the edge was rough and needs to be cut. Scott is asked to give it to the media specialist when he is finished.

At the same time about seven intermediate children from different classrooms are browsing independently in the fiction area for pleasure books. Some want a book for their reading contract (about which more in the chapter "Media Center Techniques"), others are just looking for a book to read. Harold gets help to find a *small* book for his contract. Because picture books and fiction are interfiled in this area, he does not feel that he is taking out a babyish book for his age and station. (He is 9 and in a homeroom with 3rd and 4th year students). He chooses *Mr. Jeremy Fisher* by Beatrix Potter and comes right out with it: he is really looking for a *small* book. In less than 2 weeks he reads all the Potter books and "sells" them to a number of boys in his class. He has looked up some unfamiliar words like larder, savoury, and simpleton.

In all likelihood, if it was not for the reading contract and the arrangement of the picture books, he would have missed out on Beatrix Potter.

More primary children come in for filmstrips and nonfiction books on animals. One of the girls is looking for a record that has the sound a goat makes. There is one indeed! *Barnyard Animals* produced by Droll Yankees has them all. She and her four friends happily sit down at one of the listening tables and in no time they are wired and on the farm, giggling, but completely with it. The aide tells us that Scott and Adele found what they wanted and signed their filmstrips out to show to the class.

At the other listening table six upper elementary children are listening to a pop record they have brought from home. The music teacher has given them the assignment to become acquainted with the lyrics, because she has involved them in comparing folksong lyrics with pop music lyrics. They are writing down the words, while their bodies move to the beat.

Three children of six and seven are using the card catalog. They know they will get help if they need it, but they have been shown how to find a book by using the subject catalog and they are trying their skill.

Tatti and Fred are sprawled on the rug in the story area, reading a *Sports Illustrated.* They want to cut out an ad. They can because there is an ad on the other side too. Unobtrusively a small group of children have come in from their art class to make a display of houses of all kinds and designs which they have made. The media aide has given them a large green cloth as background and they are in the process of landscaping their town with little cars and trees, in the display window which gives on one of the hallways. A suggestion that they find books on building and study prints on houses around the world by using the card catalog, to display along with their own handiwork, is enthusiastically received.

Marta and Vicki, both marvelous acrobats, are viewing film loops on gymnastics. They want to find the one with the Valdez on it. Which one would it be? *They* know what to look for and our gym teacher has told them to find it, she knows it's there because she has previewed all our gym loops.

When they have looked at all of them—we have eight— they mark the box, and sign out the loop and the classroom projector. . . . P.S.: A Valdez is a back arch walkover from a specific sitting position on the floor.

Four upper elementary children have come in, each with a picture book in one hand and a kindergartner on the other. They choose a more or less quiet spot and sit down to read a story they have prepared in advance to their charges. (See "Media Center Techniques" for a detailed description of this project.)

Nine upper elementary children are involved in collecting information for their committee reports and among four of them a discussion starts about how to find Russia in an encyclopedia. Should you look under Russia, Soviet Union, or USSR? We find that it is different in different sets! One of them straddles the fence by listing Russia before the revolution under Russia and after the revolution under USSR!

In the A-V room adjacent to the media center, but visible through a glass wall, a group of four ten- and eleven-year-olds is previewing a film, using a 16mm autoload movie projector. They project onto the white wall and, by the lights over the counter, they are taking notes from which they will prepare a ditto, with questions. The next day at a large group meeting, they will launch their new unit in social studies and the rest of the group will respond to their questions after seeing the film.

George and Andy, two upper primaries, have done a little report on the identifying marks of winter birds in their backyards. They have been working on it for about a week, adding to their collection of birds each day. They have made tracings on acetate with indelible magic marker and have colored them. They are waiting impatiently for the A-V room to become available, so that they can tape their report. They are looking through the window wall while waiting. At last the film is over. While the previewers put away the film and projector, the tape recorder is set up for these two. It is not the first time they have used it, so they do not need assistance. Before they get started one pops out quietly and turns the sign on the door to: DO NOT DISTURB.

Back at the circulation desk, ten-year-old Joy has taken over from the media aide who has repaired to the media center office where she is busily typing card sets for recordings. Joy is carding books that have been returned and placing them on a cart to be shelved. She tells me that as soon as Thayer has finished his math, he'll come to shelve and after a while they'll take turns. Thayer arrives almost immediately and begins to shelve. He does not forget to open each book before he places it on the shelf to see if Joy has put the right card in it; he loves to catch her in an error!

Suddenly there is an invasion of children who want to know what biography cake is. The day before our current reference contest had been announced on the intercom. (More about contests in "Media

Center Techniques.") The prizes will be pieces of biography cake because the contest is a biographical one, designed to make children of all levels familiar with basic biographical reference tools. It is called *Name Their Fame* (entry blanks on pages 132-134). We decide that the biography cake will be chocolate with the names of the biographees written in icing on the top. They are anxious to enter and take a contest sheet on their level.

A little more than an hour has passed since you looked inside our media center. There are other children in the carrels now. It is time for our parent volunteers to show. Before five minutes are up, they materialize. One parent is assigned to the media aide for a typing job on the periodicals which is readied for her; the other will read the shelves[8] until Joy and Thayer have to leave. She will then take the desk to card the never diminishing piles of books and other media. A look around shows that the researchers did not put all of their materials away. It is important that they be called back to clean up when their reading time in the classroom is over. When you have many pots boiling, you cannot watch all of them all of the time and some will boil over occasionally.

---

8. "Reading the shelves" is a library term meaning: to make certain that all books are in their proper places.

2

Scheduling the Use
of the Media Center

One of the most complicated steps in the establishment of a working media center is the scheduling. Time must be found for the media specialist to meet with classes, teachers, small groups of children and individual children. Many schools with library-centered arrangements begin with tightly scheduled time. The usual chronology goes something like this. Each class in the school meets with the librarian about once a week. Once the library becomes a media center, and the librarian a media specialist, schools often try to use the media center in an unscheduled, though not necessarily unstructured, manner.

THE OPEN SCHEDULE

For a media center to become truly effective, and provide all the services it can, it should be organized on what we call an open-schedule basis. We use the term open-scheduled as against closed-scheduled where each class meets weekly at a prescribed time for a prescribed period of time. The open schedule relates to concepts of need, flexibility and purpose. The scheduling has a reason, a reason which goes beyond meeting with whole classes on a weekly basis. In open scheduling, classes, groups or individuals are somewhat scheduled in their media center use, but for specific predetermined needs or purposes, and for limited numbers of times during the school year.

If the media specialist's time is scheduled on an open basis, and the teachers' and children's time is scheduled according to need, then the individualized learning which we all espouse can begin to take place, in the media center as well as the classroom. On the other hand, if the media specialist's time is totally devoted to meeting regularly scheduled whole classes, then he cannot devote his time to promoting and fulfilling the interests and needs of the teachers and children.

The media program has four major functions and organizing an open-scheduled media center is facilitated if they are kept in mind. It is the function of the media program to teach children how to procure or find media materials, how to use or utilize media materials, how to appreciate or understand media materials, and how to produce or make media materials.

ORGANIZING AROUND GOALS OF THE MEDIA PROGRAM

Goal one of the media center program, the locating or finding of media materials, is the simplest to accomplish. The children through numerous activities are shown where the materials are and how to find them.

Goal two of the media center program, the utilization of the media material, is somewhat more complicated. The skills needed to learn how to use media materials are called research skills. They range from the simple—finding a picture in the picture collection—to the difficult, taking notes from multi-sources for a written report. Research skills can be ordered and sequential, and can be mastered in a progressive approach.

Goal three of the media center program, learning to appreciate media materials, touches upon attitudes and feelings. It is important that children learn to appreciate the entire communication world and all it has to offer in a rich, full life and all it contributes to our ever growing knowledge of the world. The communication world touches upon print, pictures, paintings, music, and every form of audio-visual equipment imaginable.

Goal four of the media center program, the production of media materials, relates to presentation needs. This is, perhaps, the most difficult of the media arts. We expect that children assimilate all they have learned about a topic and reshape or reform the data into new forms. The new forms take many different shapes: written, oral or recorded reports; creative drama; pictorial representation through drawing or sketching; and the production of all in audio-visual format.

If we accept these four goals as the essence of the media center program, we can restructure our thinking about the scheduling of the media center's time and can more readily accept the concept of open scheduling. We can, if you will, make inroads into the fully scheduled media center operation, and make different arrangements of time and personnel more clearly identified with particular goals. It is important to remember that the classroom teacher is a partner in the accomplishment of all four goals. They are not the total or sole responsibility of the media specialist and his program. The classroom teacher is responsible for accomplishing the same goals. The media center and the media specialist offer her an additional arm or tool to help her achieve these ends. This is why it is essential to think always in terms of a partnership arrangement between the media specialist and each teacher. In Chapter Five suggested strategies for teacher participation in the media center program are explored. For now, we should like to explore strategies for breaking the bind of totally scheduled library or media center programs. With this in mind, let us examine each of the four goals separately.

GOAL ONE: LOCATING MATERIALS

Goal One, children must learn how to locate or find media materials. If the media center program is started early in each child's school life, most of the materials in the media center can become familiar to the children long before they leave the primary grades. We can think then of scheduling primary grades into the media center on a regular basis until each class becomes familiar with the physical layout of the media center and learns to locate all its resources without guidance. The children would also know how to use the card catalog for finding any material according to their reading abilities. They would know what the media center has to offer. Once this curriculum goal is attained there remains no reason to continue the scheduled primary class into the media center. The thing to keep in mind in the accomplishment of Goal One is that different classes will need different periods of time, and each class will cease going to the media center for its scheduled period once the goal is accomplished. This becomes the first step away from a fully scheduled media program. If goals are firmly established, then different approaches can be used for the media center's schedule.

Now, if the program has been in operation for about one year, it is safe to assume that all primary age children have mastered the skills of Goal One. Therefore, and this is important to note, it becomes unnecessary to schedule second-year students or others into the media center for the mastery of Goal One. Intermediate children should know everything about the media center, where everything is, and how to find each item. Even if the media center program is in its infancy, primary and intermediate classes need scheduling into the media center on a regular basis only until they have satisfied Goal One.

Think in terms of a full school year. Our plan shows that intermediate classes do not need media center time scheduled for Goal One, and primary classes need this scheduling only until they have mastered this goal, which will not take nearly a full school year. In an average elementary school (population 700) scheduling into the media center for mastery of Goal One will use one sixth of the media center's total time.

GOAL TWO: USING MATERIALS

Goal Two states that children must learn how to use media materials. In this category fall most library or research skills (interpreting catalog cards, note taking, film viewing, etc.). All the listening, watching, and reading skills necessary to procure information from multi-media are herein incorporated. They are an ongoing process. The skills have a sequential order. Children proceed from the mastery of the most simple (reading the titles of books) to the most complicated (preparing finished accurate solutions to problems) all through their school years. These skills are as indigenous to the classroom curriculum as they are to the media center curriculum. For this reason, the teacher must assume a shared responsibility for teaching the skills. The media center specialist and the teacher together can outline in terms of behavior each research skill. We have included a suggested list of sequential skills in Chapter Four. Once these skills are determined, the media specialist and the teacher can determine which portions of the skills program are to become the direct responsibility of the media specialist and which the direct responsibility of the classroom teacher. These skills must be taught through a cooperative, working relationship between these two professionals. Even those skills directly taught by the media specialist can only be effective if they become a consistent part of the classroom routine and are followed up carefully by the classroom teacher in her program.

The school administration can also take a role in this delegation of responsibilities and organize research skills so that some are taught in classes, some to individuals, some in the media center, and some by groups of teachers. In sequential order of difficulty these skills can be organized for presentation by the media specialist on a scheduled basis throughout the school year, one grade at a time, or one class at a time. They can be incorporated into the ongoing curriculum if the media specialist wishes. With this approach, one group of five classes can be scheduled into the media center for a period of time, while others are not; that is, for mastery of Goal Two. The other classes will be scheduled by groups at other times during the school year for accomplishment of this goal. Thus we can safely estimate, and experience has shown, that all classes will be scheduled into the media center for mastery of Goal Two at some time and this will use one sixth of the media center's total time. Units of instruction based on Goal Two should normally take some six weeks for each group of classes. We have used now one third of the media center's time for the accomplishment of Goals One and Two on a flexible basis with different classes being scheduled at different times for different reasons.

GOAL THREE: APPRECIATING MATERIALS

Goal Three, children must learn to appreciate media materials is, perhaps, the most tricky of all the goals to accomplish. It certainly is the most subtle curriculum goal to attain. If civilization stems from communication, then appreciation of this concept must be fostered in children. If indeed, life is enriched through the communication experience, then this attribute must be emphasized in the daily school life of children. We move once again quite naturally into the dual responsibility of the media specialist and the classroom teacher. Both professionals bear a responsibility for building attitudes and creating appreciations.

It would be difficult to say that we must schedule love. But, in a manner of speaking that is what we are trying to do. We want children to love, to touch, to feel, to sense, and to respect the wonders of life revealed to all of us through the communication arts. We like to encourage children to understand that the communication media are not for learning alone, but may also be for enjoyment, for pleasure—for love, if you will. One device we recommend for the media center is free browsing time. This time can be before the beginning of the official school day or at the end. It might also be during lunch and recess hours, or it might be included as a daily scheduled time during the school day, but a time known and recognized by all for browsing only. It is necessary that browsing time be included somewhere in the media center program on a daily basis.

This is the time when children, encouraged by their classroom teacher, come as individuals to the center for no specific purpose. It is free time—time for children to explore, to find, to touch, to look, to listen, to sense, to reject. This type of scheduling should be arranged for once or twice a day. The child, with the teacher's approval, comes when he wishes. He can use this time to find anything he wishes, totally unrelated to his class curriculum; he can take what he wants back to his class, back to the center, or just leave it. It is during these times that the media specialist is a guide, not a director. He stays in the background. His influence is gentle, subtle, indirect. He helps only if he is asked.

The media specialist can encourage the appreciation of communication skills in more direct ways. He can introduce units of interest for all children or some of the children all through the school year. For example, he can introduce a poetry unit for the very young for a few weeks. During this unit of study, he would schedule classes for visitations to the center for a few weeks at a time. The media specialist, mindful of Goal Three, can introduce specific units of study for different groups of classes at different times during the school year. Different types of appreciation activities can be started by the classroom teacher and followed up in the media center. In this case, individual classes would be scheduled into the media center for short periods of time for just these activities.

We estimate that another sixth of the media center's time will be used for the accomplishment of Goal Three. We have now used one half of the media center's time for the accomplishment of Goals One, Two, and Three in our open-scheduled plan.

GOAL FOUR: PRODUCING MATERIALS

Goal Four, teaching children how to produce media materials, is creatively the most exciting of all. Children will be taught to prepare their materials for presentation. In other words, children having learned to locate, use, and appreciate, must learn how to prepare their own media materials for use and appreciation by others. Most media production originates with some problem solution in the classroom curriculum. The problem stems from units of study or interest manifested through the classroom curriculum. Youngsters, committees, small groups, and sometimes entire classes amass all the data they need for solving problems, and must at this point become involved in methods and techniques for preparing their material for presentation to others. How can they transmit what they know to others? The possibilities are limitless.

Presentations can be written, oral, modelled, or pictorial. They can be live. They can be two or three dimensional. They can be with or without words, or sounds, or music. They can be with or without acting or drama. What we are saying is that all the media materials the children have utilized in data collection can be produced or reproduced on an original basis for presentation purposes. The children have first to master the skills of preparing a good written or oral report before going on to more complex and original creations with audio-visual media. Many skills need teaching if children are to learn to prepare all types of media presentation programs. What we suggest is that small groups of children or individual children be moved to the media center on a scheduled basis once they have reached the data collection stage. In short-range scheduled sessions, media production can be taught to children as they are ready for them or see a need for them. The classroom teacher decides when a child or group of children is ready for media preparation. We estimate that another sixth of the media center's time will be devoted to this type of activity for the accomplishment of Goal Four.

We have then accounted for a total of two-thirds of the time used by the media center for the accomplishment of Goals One through Four. We allow in our plan roughly one sixth of the media specialist's time for his own preparation and review of material and schedules, and conferences with teachers to coordinate plans. This leaves another sixth of the media center's time completely unscheduled, for random use in further refinement of Goals One through Four as the need arises. These situations usually arise and they relate to individual children, or small groups of children working on similar problems, or those who need individual remediation or enrichment in media skills.

Incidentally, if supervision is available in the media center, one must remember that the media specialist can make fine use of his time by providing some of his instruction directly in the classrooms (where feasible), leaving the media center open for other children to work as individuals or in small groups.

THE WEEKLY PLAN

Media specialists operating on this type of open schedule find they can plan ahead for the next week's program. Each week (on Friday preferably) an open schedule is prepared for the following week and distributed to the faculty. The schedule would show which classes are meeting the following week for the accomplishment of Goals One through Three. It also shows completely unscheduled time for teachers to send children to the center for meeting Goals Two through Four on an individual or small group basis.

Figure 2-1 is a typical open schedule during the first year of operation. There are three sessions of large group instruction with intermediate classes (Classes L and P). The skills are Goal Two skills and the area of study is South America. Two primary classes (Classes C and D) are still being seen for Goal One activities which they have not sufficiently mastered, although other primary classes have completed these skills. Six classes (Classes Q to V) are being seen individually. They are in the midst of Goal Three activities on a unit of study initiated by the media specialist on Afro-American cultural contributions. Browsing time is included for each day. All other times are open. They may be used for individual children working on projects and problems relating to their curriculum with emphasis on Goals Two, Three, or Four. This open time is also utilized by the media specialist for consultation with teachers for future plans and for his multitudinous clerical and organizational duties.

A second- and third-year media schedule always shows more open time. Children have mastered more skills and are more and more ready for individual or small committee assignments in the media center. Teachers are given a copy of the week's media schedule and can readily see for themselves when they can send children to the media center without interrupting other children or the media specialist. They can also see when the media specialist is free to consult with them. The schedule must be published each week, because each week is different. This is the essence of flexible open scheduling.

This operational plan becomes routine once firmly established in the habits of each teacher's weekly planning. Teachers find they can plan their own weekly programs with recognition of media center

Elmwood School   **Media Center Schedule**   **Week of Jan. 3, 19__**

Hours	Monday	Tuesday	Wednesday	Thursday	Friday
9:00 / 10:00	Classes L - P Large Group Goal 2		Classes L - P Large Group Goal 2		Classes L - P Large Group Goal 2
10:00 / 11:00					
11:00 / 12:00		Class C Goal 1		Class D Goal 1	
12:00- 1:00	LUNCH and RECESS FREE BROWSING TIME				
1:00- 2:00	Class Q Goal 3	Class R Goal 3	Class S Goal 3	Class T Goal 3	Class U Goal 3
2:00- 3:00			Class V Goal 3		

Figure 2-1

open time that their children can use as the curriculum needs of their own program dictate.

MORE OPEN TIME

One final word: the skilled media specialist can make the program more viable if he plans to present certain activities, skills or projects to large groups rather than to individual children, small groups or classes. Many of the skills which need teaching lend themselves naturally and easily to large group instruction. The media specialist can arrange his schedule so that some of these skills can be taught on a large group basis. Reinforcement and enrichment activities with smaller groups can follow large group presentation. The discriminate use of large group instruction by the media specialist creates more open time in the media center schedule for independent and small group work. In certain instances, the media specialist can give his lessons in a classroom.

There are skills which can be taught in the classroom as well as in the media center. The use of this scheme, as previously mentioned, also permits more independent use of the media center by children, provided there is adequate supervision—which means additional personnel. Large group instruction and classroom based lessons are two suggestions for creating more open time in the schedule for the children's individual and small group work time in the center. The media center becomes a coming and going place. Action all the time. Groups moving in and out. Individuals coming and going. Lessons taking place and independent research taking place and both at the same time. All of this can be happening, but only through the utilization of an open schedule for the use of the media center. It is the open schedule which helps to free both the media center and the media specialist for more creative and individualized work with children.

The best strategy for opening time in the schedule for the media specialist is to free him from as much clerical detail work as possible. This can be accomplished through the use of para-professionals or trained volunteer parents.

3

Curriculum for a
Media Center

DEVELOPMENT OF GOALS

How a media center curriculum evolves from the four goals outlined in Chapter Two is best shown by examples of classroom units and related media skills learnings. Some of these skills are best taught in concert with a subject that is current in the classroom. Others can be successfully taught directly. The media specialist discusses these skills with the classroom teacher and together they decide the how and when.

In order to teach these media skills it is suggested that media be purchased in the following broad areas, which are usually studied in most elementary schools:

in SOCIAL STUDIES

Kindergarten: Home and school
First year: The neighborhood
Second year: The local community and county
Third year: Greater urban or rural area
Fourth year: The home state and the U.S.
Fifth year: The Americas
Sixth year: The Eastern Hemisphere

in SCIENCE

The following science units are studied at all levels in different degrees of depth:

Weather
Electricity and magnetism

Plants and animals
The solar system
Keeping healthy
Ecology and conservation
Machines

in LANGUAGE ARTS

Fiction and nonfiction media on all levels, including

primary: Easy-to-read books and filmstrips
Folk and fairy tales
Picture books in all media
Poetry
Simple nonfiction books
Easy-to-read biographies
intermediate: Interesting fiction such as: science fiction,
adventure and mystery stories
Folklore
Poetry
Biography

GOAL I: LOCATING MEDIA MATERIALS

On the primary levels, the most important skills are: finding out what a media center is for; where all the different media are; and learning how to handle simple media and their accompanying hardware carefully, while becoming an independent user and borrower. Translated into a list of sequential skills this means that the primary child will be exposed to the following:

Borrowing and returning of materials
Locating picture books
Locating "beginning to read" books
Locating folk and fairy tales
Locating books on favorite nonfiction topics
Knowing where to find filmstrips
Knowing where to find records and tapes
Learning to use a previewer
Learning to use a record player with headphones
Learning to use a tape recorder
Learning to interpret a filmstrip or other visual from the
pictures
Learning the parts of a picture book and a simple nonfiction
book

Care of books and other media
Care of equipment
How to reserve a book

MEDIA CENTER KINDERGARTEN CURRICULUM

Where the media center is in the school, what it is for and what it offers, is taught inductively at the kindergarten level by making arrangements for semi-monthly story-telling times, when use is made of all the different media that are suitable. The program is varied to include poetry, folk and fairy tales, simple science materials, songs, riddles, and games. The emphasis is on enjoying, listening and participating. On this level enjoyment is a skill that needs to be acquired by many children.

Throughout the year the kindergarten teachers make it a point to send different children to the media center, whenever an answer is needed to a question which cannot readily be answered in the classroom. The answer is found for them, marked with a bookmark in several books; a filmstrip on the subject is added whenever possible and the children return to their room convinced that the media center is "full of answers!" Small groups of children are frequently sent to the media center to choose picture books for the teacher to use with them. They also return books no longer needed in the classroom. At this age they do not yet borrow books in their own name to take home. Exceptions are made in individual cases, when the teacher recommends it.

First Skills Unit

The first-year students are taught directly: where things are; what they are called; how to borrow and return a book; and care of books and other media. Their first media center unit takes three weeks to complete and is comprised of four visits to the media center, one visit of the media specialist to the classroom and one large group meeting in the auditorium.

The first visit is a tour of the fiction and story-telling area. Labels on brightly colored oaktag in primary printing are attached to those shelf sections of interest to the children. During the tour the signs are read aloud, children who can read them may do so, a story is chosen from a section of their choice and is enjoyed. A second visit the same week covers the nonfiction area of the media center, labeled to indicate the location of favorite subjects like dinosaurs, animals, and stars. An A-V story hour follows on a nonfiction topic. The next week the media specialist visits the classroom with enough bookcards for each child. Using the overhead projector and a transparency of an actual bookcard with real names on it (Illustration 3-1), the children are shown how to write their name, the date and their class letter in the right places on the bookcard. The overhead projector is left in the classroom for children to write on the transparency until everyone has had a turn. The teacher follows this lesson up by noting the date on the blackboard every day in the same manner as on the bookcard (9-16). Every day the children practice writing date, name and class letter on each other's bookcards in teams of two; they also use the overhead in teams of two to practice.

The second meeting of this week is a visit to the media center to hear *Rosa Too Little* by Felt, a story of a little Puerto Rican girl who was determined to learn to write her name so she could borrow books from the New York Public Library. During the third week a film on book care[1] is shown to all during one large group meeting in the auditorium. After the film a transparency of four book-care bookmarks is projected. The book-care poems on the bookmarks are read aloud. Each teacher will receive a box of these bookmarks to hand out as "passes" the first four times each child comes individually to the media center to borrow a book (Illustration 3-2). The bookmark in his hand will identify him as a first borrower to the media specialist; it will reinforce the book-care film for the child and he will learn the use of a bookmark. Perhaps his parents will read him the book-care poem again when he brings it home in his first book!

The last visit of this series is actually an initiation ceremony. Each class comes as a group to the media center where over a lighted candle a library pledge is said in verse, which repeats briefly some of the information covered before. On the table with the candle two rolls of primary lined newsprint are taped down. With a red magic marker, each child again writes the date, his name and his class letter. (Divide the group in half to make it go faster!) Then each child is given a letter (Illustration 3-3) to take home to his parents which states that he or she is now a full-fledged member of the media center. Not until his parents and he have signed the letter and the child has returned it, is he permitted to borrow from the media center. After this introductory sequence of lessons the children come in small groups of no more than five to the media center at the teacher's discretion. When they come they are shown individually

---

1. *Libraries Are for Sharing.* Newenhouse, 1965; color, 11 minutes.

E

Seuss, Dr.
The cat in the hat comes back

DATE	BORROWER'S NAME	
10-22	Richard S.	B
10-29	Keit Stein	B
1-30	Janet P.	C
11-18	Steven W.	I
11-26	Paul H	B
12-9	Mark	F
12-11	Peter M	C
	Karl H	e

Illustration 3-1.

The way you care
The way you share
The way you keep
Books neat,
Will make
Borrowing a treat
For everyone
Who picks them up
And takes them
Home to read.
When finished,
Do remember
To return them
The next day!
For you someone
Will do the same,
That's the way
To play
The library game.

When you read me,
Please treat me
With kindness
And care.

If turned
At the corner,
My pages won't
Get "worner"
Than they
Now are!

Please save me
From the snow,
From rain,
Mud and
Hands dirty.

When I go,
Back again,
I'd like to
Be as "purty,"
As when you
Took me out;
Without a
Single stain.

Please keep
Me away
From little
Scribblers!

Near puppy
Nibblers
Don't leave
Me lay!

Illustration 3-2.

ELMWOOD MEDIA CENTER
October 4, 19____

Dear Parent,

This week your child has officially become a member of the
ELMWOOD MEDIA CENTER by participating in a candle lighting
ceremony during which he said this pledge:

> I promise to treat our books with care,
> To return them neat, for others to share.
> I'll keep them dry, when outside it is wet,
> I'll keep them high, away from my pet.
> I'll read them and return them
> As soon as I am done:
> For you to borrow, tomorrow,
> And have a lot of fun.

Signed:_____   _____
                        first name   initial of
                                                          last name

- -

After saying this pledge, your child solemnly wrote his first name
and initial of his last name on a scroll. This is what he will have to do
on a bookcard each time he borrows a book from our Media Center.
Our next M.C. lesson will be devoted to teaching this skill. After that
he will be allowed to borrow one book at a time to take home. We
do not limit him to a once a week visit, nor do we censor his choice.
Making a "wrong" choice is part of learning. At the discretion of his
teacher, your child will come to exchange his book when it is
finished. "A book is due, when you are through" is our motto.
Books are *over*due when they have been kept more than one month.
(On the date slip, the last stamped date is the date it was borrowed.)

To help reinforce what your child has learned, please say the
pledge with him once more and have *him* sign it. Send back the top
half of this letter with him to his teacher.

I wish you both much shared enjoyment of our Media Center
books and thank you for your help in making a responsible media
user of your child.

Sincerely,

Miriam H. Wexler, Librarian

Illustration 3-3.
52

how to complete the borrowing transaction by filing their bookcard in a card sorter by first letter of the author's last name, as printed on the card. This teaches a beginning alphabetizing skill and a selective reading skill, the identification of an author's last name on a card which includes a title, a first name and many other symbols. Identifying an author's last name as the name before the comma on the first line of a bookcard prepares the child for locating an author's name on a catalog card when he locates books in the subject catalog later in the year.

Because this first skills unit has been thoroughly planned with the teacher, she will reinforce the skills in the classroom whenever possible. She never reads a story aloud without turning to the title page to read the title and author's name, pointing to each. After a while she forgets deliberately, to see if someone will catch her. If no one does she asks: "What did I forget?" When a book has particularly outstanding illustrations she mentions the name of the illustrator by looking for it on the title page.

It is recommended that all first-year children visit the media center to exchange books as soon as they have finished one. In the beginning they are supervised when they write their bookcards and file them. They are given free reign and their choices are never censored; they are given help if they ask or look helpless. Eventually discrimination develops by trial and error; as soon as a child begins to read he will look for books he is able to read. Until that time, what he needs most may be the prestige of carrying a big book around! Everything is fair game, except the unabridged dictionaries!

Second Skills Unit

In their second skills unit, first-year students learn to handle uncomplicated media, such as filmstrips and recordings as well as the hardware necessary for their use. These manipulative skills are taught in class size and small groups by prearrangement with the classroom teacher. An introductory lesson for one whole class group covers basic rules governing the use of the hardware, the locations of the software and its handling. Record players and tape recorders are introduced at one time: four groups in one class listen simulta- neously to a short selection on tape and on a record. The selections are different and could be related to an ongoing classroom unit. The media specialist uses a tape recorder to sum up, asking each group to tell what they have heard. It is taped right then and there, showing in this fashion both uses of the tape recorder. A playback of each group is listened to by all. The tape is given to the classroom teacher to play again. For subsequent instruction the classes are broken into small groups of six and at prearranged times each group has a small group experience with a filmstrip viewer, a record player and a tape recorder.[2] Each child learns individually to handle each piece of equipment and clean up when he is finished. The classroom teacher follows up throughout the rest of the school year, by sending children to the media center, individually or in small groups with a note to use a filmstrip, tape or record on a particular subject current in the classroom. In this way the children become increasingly familiar with software and hardware and learn to report on tape what they have listened to or seen. Twelve weeks are set aside for these two skills units; three weeks of teaching and three weeks of follow up for each unit, a minimum amount of time to cover the material with a group of at least 125 primary children.

GOAL II: UTILIZATION OF MEDIA

Primary Levels

In the second and third school year emphasis is on the following simple research skills:

Understanding in greater depth the difference between fiction and nonfiction

Understanding the difference between the arrangement of fiction and nonfiction

The ability to select pertinent material from a book through the use of the table of contents

The ability to select pertinent frames from a filmstrip, passages from a recording and pictures from books or picture files for use in a simple oral report

Learning to use a simple encyclopedia to answer a specific question

Selecting pertinent materials through use of the subject card in the card catalog for all media

The above skills are taught informally as they are needed. A varied and interesting classroom environment provides the matrix for many individual and group research projects. A teacher with many different kinds of pets in his room sets the stage for inquiry and

---

2. When an 8 or super 8 mm movie camera is available, an instructional film made in your own media center with primary children and your own equipment is an invaluable aid.

discovery. What to feed the turtle a child has found on the road can lead to a classroom unit on how reptiles gather food and what animals prey on them. This may lead to an investigation of the eating habits of many other animals and an understanding of the balance of nature and ecology. A cottontail rabbit leads a child to find out all he can about rabbits and hares, after which he reads all the rabbit stories in the media center he can get hold of. In the end he writes his own rabbit story, incorporates all he has absorbed about rabbits and presents it to many classes with tape recorder and illustrations on transparencies.

Reports in Various Media

The teachers on this level emphasize simple reports consisting of oral presentation, or presentation on tape, illustrated by selected frames of a filmstrip and pertinent passages of a book, with pictures shown on the opaque projector, the showing of a silent 8mm film loop by a child with commentary created by him, or a combination of any of these techniques.

When the need to find materials arises, card catalog skills are taught informally to individuals or small groups of no more than five and are at first limited to the subject catalog, because most children need to find materials by subject. The media specialist is always in close contact with the teacher and small group instruction in card catalog skills is easily arranged for those who are ready for it. As to "research" the teacher helps by making the questions to be researched as specific as possible, writing them on a slip of paper which the child brings with him to the media center.

Intermediate Levels

In the fourth, fifth and sixth school years the primary research skills are refined, intensified and taught in greater depth. Refinement and depth are accomplished when the skills listed below are added to the child's repertoire:

Using indexes in encyclopedias and other reference sources
Note taking (on index cards)
Documentation of sources
Comparing of sources
Outlining
Using an index to periodicals
Compiling a report from notes taken

Constructing a cross-media bibliography
Using author, subject and title cards in card catalog for all
media

Sample Unit in Social Studies

The sample unit which follows is used with an intermediate group comprised of fourth- and fifth-year children. It incorporates all but two of the skills in the course of a year's work, gradually building on previous accomplishments and expecting that all fourth- and fifth-year students will have successfully added these to their tools, except for bibliography making and using a periodical index. Those who can should by all means try these last two, but they can safely be left to the last school year.

This social studies unit on the U.S. is taught concurrently with a science unit on ecology and conservation. The social studies unit which covers the geography, anthropology, sociology, economy and history (biographical approach) becomes the vehicle to teach the above media and study skills. The fifth-year students in this group (Group I) covered all the aspects of this unit the previous year and are now going to apply what they have learned and are learning this year about ecology and conservation by concentrating on man-made urban problems in 15 key cities. The fourth-year students (Group II) will follow the usual curriculum, beginning in the same 15 cities and branching out to the surrounding states of which these cities are the urban centers. At the completion of the unit which will take the better part of a year, both groups will translate their learnings into an action program to be applied to their local metropolitan suburban county of Rockland, N.Y.

As the unit will begin in the city for both groups, the teacher decides to launch it with the film *The Changing City* (Churchill Films).[3] She prepares for the showing of the film by devoting her first lesson (with the whole class) to a discussion of cities which have disappeared from the face of the earth. She has listed these cities on a ditto and an overhead transparency (p. 57). The class conjectures as to possible causes for the disappearance of these cities. The discussion yields many possibilities: earthquakes, floods, tidal waves, hurricanes, tornadoes, encroachment of jungles, war, fire, disease, and polluted water supply. The teacher explains that to find out why the cities (listed on the ditto) disappeared, the encyclopedia is the

3. This is a free film which can be obtained in New York State from the film library at S.U.N.Y., College of Forestry, Syracuse, N.Y.

POMPEII disappeared because_____

_____

Source:_____,_____,_____,_____

      title   Volume Page   Copyright date

KNOSSOS disappeared because_____

_____

Source: _____,_____,_____,_____

     t.   V.   p.   c.

ANGKOR VAT disappeared because_____

_____

Source:_____,_____,_____,_____

     t.   V.   p.   c.

HERCULANEUM disappeared because_____

_____

Source:_____,_____,_____,_____

     t.   V.   p.   c.

MACHU PICCHU disappeared because_____

_____

Source:_____,_____,_____,_____

     t.   V.   p.   c.

TROY disappeared because_____

_____

Source:_____,_____,_____,_____

     t.   V.   p.   c.

ATLANTIS disappeared because_____

_____

Source:_____,_____,_____,_____

     t.   V.   p.   c.

CHICHEN ITZA disappeared because_____

_____

Source:_____,_____,_____,_____

     t.   V.   p.   c.

PRIENE disappeared because_____

_____

Source:_____,_____,_____,_____

     t.   V.   p.   c.

most useful reference tool. She requires that for this reference assignment the children use the encyclopedias in the media center; that for each city a different encyclopedia (title) must be used[4] and that each answer must be documented on the source line under each city's name on the ditto. She demonstrates how to do it on the overhead with the first city listed on the ditto: *Pompeii.* A week is allowed to complete this information. The following week the collected information is summarized and outlined together with the class and organized into two groups: I. Cities which perished through natural disasters, and II. Cities which were wiped out through man-made catastrophies.

By referring to the T.V. program "1985" it is pointed out that many U.S. cities and whole areas of the country could be wiped out by man's manipulation of his environment and by his lack of understanding and concern. This leads to *Key Question #1:* For what reasons could cities of today become unfit to live in and have to be abandoned?

Note Taking from Various Media

This is an ideal moment to introduce the class to note taking and an ideal medium is a film, because copying is not possible in the dark and listening and observation skills must be sharp to recall the information. The film is viewed with the teacher and media specialist present. Following the film the media specialist shows how to take notes on a 6x4 index card (reproduced on the transparency maker) to answer Key Question #1 on the source-note card below, eliciting the responses from the class.

Source - Film. *The Changing City.* Churchill,
              media   title   publisher @date
Subject: MAN-MADE CITY PROBLEMS
notes: Crowded conditions, ghettoes, slums, transportation, electric power, air pollution, water supply, education, crime, drugs, recreation spaces, race problems

---

4. Reason: the class should get as many different experiences as possible with as many different encyclopedias as possible, to observe their arrangement, reading level, and other differences.

The media specialist then gives examples of two source-note cards on just one of the problems covered by the film: *Garbage Disposal.*

Source - Film, The Changing City. Churchill.
    media   title   publisher ©date

Subject: GARBAGE DISPOSAL
    A. Household garbage
notes: Most big cities have more garbage than they can handle. In some cities it is towed out to sea and dumped. In others it is buried and used as landfill. Too much garbage, like bottles and cans, does not rot away causing litter.

and

Source - Film, The Changing City. Churchill.
Subject: GARBAGE DISPOSAL
    B. Industrial garbage
notes: Many factories dump waste into rivers. This loads the water with chemicals which kill fish. Sometimes hot water which was used to cool machines is dumped in the rivers. The temperature of the river rises which kills river wildlife.

The advantage of the source-note card in note taking is that the cards can be organized by subject in any desired outline; the subtopics can be reshuffled at will and so can the sources, by media, by author or by title. The media specialist points out that no matter what the source, the notes are always taken in the same way. If the source is a book the author's name is placed in front of the title and the page numbers used come after the copyright date. The teacher follows up the note taking lesson in other subject areas, using the same method and checking on the format until every child has it down pat.

Now the class is divided into two groups. Until the winter holidays Group I will do research on man-made urban problems, culminating in committee reports on related problems. Each child in Group I selects one of the problems suggested by the film and begins to take notes on his topic, using a different type of media each time he comes to the media center. He is required to use at least three of the different media which follow: encyclopedias, books, filmstrips, sound filmstrips, recordings, film loops, pamphlets—one at a time. The media specialist gives help in the media center. The teacher checks on individual progress in the classroom. When a good start is made (about two weeks should be sufficient), the teacher calls Group I together and asks *Key Question #2:* Which of the problems you are working on can be grouped together because they belong together? After, discussion committees on related problems are formed. The children have decided that all man-made problems can be put into four groups:

> I. Natural resource problems
> II. Human resource problems
> III. Population problems (conflicts)
> IV. Technological problems

Each child now joins the committee which covers the problem he is working on. Actually this is the children's first experience in outlining as a group activity. After another three weeks or so an oral interim report is made on each group of problems from the source-note cards. The group leader is responsible for the arrangement of the subtopics; the teacher organizes the committee topics in a logical sequence. Showing the total outline as the children report (on the overhead) will make them realize that they themselves created the overall structure of the report—which is called *outlining.* As the group reports, appropriate illustrations are projected; maps have been made and produced as transparencies, the committee that worked on technological problems has dramatized its reports and called it "Where will you be when the lights go out?"

The children in Group II meanwhile are working on map skills and will culminate this part of their work with a planned trip in winter, spring, summer or fall to one of the cities listed below. They have the choice of season and itinerary; may visit three places of interest on the way; may travel by car, train or air, but must calculate their total mileage one way. They will plan a week's stay at a "friend's"[5] house taking into account indoor and outdoor activities based on the prevailing weather for which statistics are available, during the time of the pretend visit. The children in Group II use all available media to collect their travel and trip information including the following films on cities which have been borrowed at no cost by the media specialist:[6]

---

5. The "friend" may be a real friend, relative or acquaintance or a person known to someone in the school, who will be inclined to answer one letter.

6. Obtainable from Association Films Inc., 600 Grand Ave, Ridgefield, N.J.

Design for a City (Philadelphia); *Mood of Three Cities* (Dallas, San Francisco, Chicago); *My City* (New York); *Profiles: Philadelphia, San Diego, Cleveland; Rochester, a City of Quality* and *New York.*

In the interim, during language arts the classroom teacher has been working on letter writing. About a month before the Christmas holidays, the children in Group I write letters to those city agencies, located through telephone directories,[7] which have jurisdiction over the problem they are studying; while the children in Group II write letters to their pretend hosts, preparing them for their arrival and giving them a tentative plan in outline form for their visit. Both groups will use these same cities for their projects:

ATLANTA	CLEVELAND	NEW ORLEANS	PITTSBURGH
BOSTON	DALLAS	NEW YORK	ST LOUIS
BURBANK	KANSAS CITY	NEWARK	SEATTLE
CHICAGO	LOS ANGELES	PHILADELPHIA	WASHINGTON, D.C.

After the holidays the children in Group I concentrate on their city and the problem they have chosen to investigate before. Their previously gained background knowledge of the problem will be of great help to them in their writing what might be called for lack of a better term a "position paper." In developing the outline for their position paper, they will have to check and take notes on how the same problem has been treated in other cities and even in other countries. At this time the *Abridged Readers Guide to Periodicals* is introduced to Group I children who need to find magazine articles on current practices related to their problem. The position paper will outline the extent of the problem in the city of their choice; will include suggestions on how to deal with the problem constructively, or develop an original solution within the realm of possibility. The position paper is an individual activity and is presented in whatever form best suits the child and the topic.

The children in Group II have had a most enjoyable pretend visit to their chosen city. Because they were not actually there they do not have to write a thank you letter! They are now ready to branch out from the city of their choice for a survey of the state and a group of surrounding states. The child who went to Atlanta becomes responsible for Georgia and the neighboring states of Florida, Alabama, Mississippi; the child who visited Boston investigates the New England states of Massachusetts, Maine, New Hampshire, Ver-

---

7. Obtainable from the N.Y. Telephone Co. at no cost.

mont and Rhode Island. All children in Group II have to find the answers to three *Key Questions:*

In what way is your city important to the neighboring states?

Your area has mineral resources, wildlife resources and human resources. Choose one group of these resources and find out if they are being conserved or wasted. Tell how.

How does the treatment of these resources, good or bad, affect the other resources in the area? If they are being conserved are they being conserved properly without harming other resources? If they are being wasted what could be done to stop waste and begin proper conservation?

The children in Group II are encouraged to draw up a practical program in outline form, if their situation calls for it.

When this work is completed by both groups, we are ready for the final *Key Question:* Do some of the problems you have been studying occur also in our own suburban Rockland County? What problems do we have right here in our own environment? The children identify some of the problems and find others by digging through a pile of back issues of the local newspaper. They take notes avidly. The whole class together outlines an action program in which they can participate locally. Again they work in committees formed around related problems. They have become aware of the waste they create themselves. They begin their action program in the classroom by salvaging things they used to throw out, like large scraps of construction paper; unused note paper is collected and used for scrap paper: pencil stubs are collected and donated to the media center (and gratefully received); buttons, hair barrettes, broken jewelry, erasers, pieces of crayon and other sundries are collected and reused as raw materials for collages, constructions, mobiles and other class projects. A regular monthly schoolground clean-up day is proposed. They decide to let local government officials know how they feel about waste and pollution. In letters to the editor of the local paper they let the whole community know how they feel. They decide to wage a campaign at home to persuade their parents to take positive, specific steps for conservation. They coin slogans against waste, for a cleaner Hudson River, for beautification, and display them in store windows. A program for broadcasting on the local radio station is prepared. They open each school day with the reading of a brief nature poem, which a different child each day finds in the media center. They collect them and resolve that a different person will read one of them every Monday morning over the intercom the following school year; a truly poetic ending to a most satisfying year's work.

GOAL III: APPRECIATING MEDIA MATERIALS

Primary Levels

Understanding and appreciation of anything at all is the result of enjoyment. It is rather artificial to treat this part of the media program separately from the skills program, because in practice they go hand in hand. To a small child especially, mastering a skill like borrowing on his own, viewing and handling equipment is as enjoyable as listening to a good story, well told—perhaps even more! However, one does not live by skills alone and a well-balanced media program of course includes a good measure of enjoyable literary experiences with all media. For greatest enjoyment and appreciation, use that medium as the messenger which most effectively expresses the subject.

Enjoyment comes when one of the media leads to another, enlarging the scope and vision and inviting comparison. Appreciation grows with understanding of the possibilities and limitations of the various media. Enjoyment is complete with the appreciation of the different modes of communication as forms of art and the arts as forms of communication.

On a primary level, such experiences as:

Picture-book story hours
Live story telling
Impromptu dramatization of favorite stories
Professional dramatization of folk tales
A-V story times and "radio" story times
Meeting favorite authors and illustrators in person and on film and corresponding with them
Guided reading, through a specially created reading recipe and viewing and listening experiences.

will set the stage. The media specialist is the producer. He has learned how best to exploit the potential of each of the media. When he wishes to reach more than 25 children with a picture-book story, he uses the best of the media for this purpose: the iconographic picture-book films and sound filmstrips, made by Morton Schindel's Weston Woods Studios—because "a book is not a group or distance medium. Its words were never intended to be orated to a vast audience and its illustrations were created for children to examine at leisure, down to the minutest detail."[8]

Because live story telling is most effective when the story-teller has command of his audience with his eyes and his voice, a small (25) group is best. The school intercom can do double service as a radio station for regularly scheduled story hours for large groups, primary and intermediate. There are many advantages to this medium. Memorization is not necessary. Sound effects are possible. Taping the story can be done at leisure in advance. Voice effects enhance the story. Children can do it in small groups, each one vocally dramatizing a character in the story.

A sequence of stories in picture books, on filmstrips, on films, and on recordings or tape, on T.V., in poetry and art, all dealing with the same subject, for example *rabbits* at springtime, gives children a chance to appreciate differences in treatment through illustrations, renditions, content and format. Enjoyment for a kindergartner is to be picked up by an older child and taken to the media center to be read to. Short annotated bibliographies are provided for teachers who wish to read aloud to their classes. Simple puzzle contests are an ongoing activity in the media center. Sample puzzles are posted on the puzzle bulletin board. They are fun and there is a prize! (a piece of homemade cake or candy bar). The puzzles reinforce skills previously taught and often also serve as reading lists, when successfully completed. Everyone who completes a puzzle successfully gets a prize. For examples of primary level puzzles, see in Chapter Six the sections: "Where Are the Titles?" (for beginners) page 150; "The Magic Number 3" page 149; and "Name Their Fame Contest" (for beginners) page 132.

Intermediate Levels

Understanding and appreciation of communication on the intermediate levels is brought about more by participating in the communication arts than by being mostly on the receiving end. A subtle change in appreciation takes place as soon as the children become producers of media and participants in media productions, whether it is a simple picture book or a multi-media wrap-up of a classroom unit.

---

8. Morton Schindel, "The Picture Book Projected," *School Library Journal*, February 1968, pp. 46-47.

These activities in which the intermediate children take part include:

Live story telling by children to other groups
Dramatization of folktales and book scenes
Creating picture books for younger children
Corresponding with favorite authors and inviting them to take part in book programs
Preparing a picture-book story to read to a younger child
Making media center displays
Reviewing new books and other media for the school paper
Free and guided reading for enjoyment
Film making as creative expression
Puzzle and contest activities related to media and media skills

The Reading Contract

From all that went before, it is clear that direct teaching in this context is impossible. However, just as it is possible to create an environment inviting to discovery by having many pets in the classroom, it is quite simple to set the scene for deeper involvement in the communication arts by using the "Reading Contract" as a curtain raiser. (For samples of Reading Contracts see pages 66-72.)

What is the Reading Contract? It is the foundation of the supplementary reading program. It is designed to ensure that children who do not read much for pleasure, will—by mandating that all children on intermediate levels 11-20 select and read at least one supplementary (trade) book for each reading level they complete. The reading teacher allows time during the reading period for the selection of a book in the media center, the reading of it and the completion of the Reading Contract. The classroom teacher allows time for the reading of supplementary books and completion of Reading Contracts only as an extra activity during free time. (See pages 66-72.) In other words, supplementary reading in the classroom is one of the many other activities on each teacher's list of independent classroom activities. Frequently the teacher will send a child to the media specialist to check on and approve his reading contract. This gives the media specialist a chance to discuss the book with the child and recommend another. At testing time each child brings his completed Reading Contracts with him.

From the seven different Reading Contracts a teacher of fifth- and sixth-year students has observed that many children have read books on the theme *courage*. This gives him an opening to set the scene for

SUPPLEMENTARY READING CONTRACT

Reading Instructional Levels 11—16   *Fiction*

Name_____ Reading Class_____
Reading Level_____Regular Class_____Date_____
Title of Book_____
Author of Book_____#of pages_____
Publisher of Book_____Date of publication__

Please complete all the information above. Answer all the questions below except the last one, which you may or may not complete. You may use extra paper if you do not have enough room on this sheet.

———————————

Characterization—People, Animals

Tell me all about one person in this book. Describe what he or she looks like.

Describe how he or she acts.

Describe how other people or animals in the story feel about this person.

Tell why you liked or disliked this person or animal.

SUPPLEMENTARY READING CONTRACT

Reading Instructional Levels 11–16   *Fiction*

Name_____   Reading Class_____

Reading Level_____Regular class_____Date_____

Title of Book_____

Author of Book_____# of pages_____

Publisher of Book_____Date of publication_____

Please complete all the information above and answer all the
questions below. You may use extra paper if you do not have
enough room on this sheet.

_____

Scenery (Local Color)

Where does story take place?
(geographical identification)

Find a passage in the story that described the scenery well.
Copy it down in quotations. Draw a picture in color of the
scenery.

Would you like to visit this kind of place? Tell why it appeals
to you.

SUPPLEMENTARY READING CONTRACT

Reading Instructional Levels 11-16   *Fiction*

Name_____ Reading Class_____

Reading Level_____Regular Class_____Date_____

Title of Book_____

Author of Book_____# of pages_____

Publisher of Book_____Date of publication_____

Please complete all the information above and answer all the questions below. You may use extra paper if you do not have enough room on this sheet.

Message (Theme)

Tell in your own words what the author was trying to say in the story.

Do you think the author wanted us to understand something after we read the book? What was it?

Do you think the author did a good job in weaving his message into the story? Tell why.

Do you feel differently about things or people since you've read this book? Do you act differently? Tell how.

SUPPLEMENTARY READING CONTRACT

Reading Instructional Levels 11—16   *Fiction*

Name_____ Reading Class_____

Reading Level_____Regular Class_____Date_____

Title of Book_____

Author of Book_____# of pages_____

Publisher of Book_____Date of Publication_____

Please complete all the information above and answer all the questions below. You may use extra paper if you do not have enough room on this sheet.

_____

Story Line—Plot

Describe in your own words the story (plot) of the book from the beginning to the crisis or problem.

What was the crisis or problem in this book?

How was the crisis or problem in this book solved? Can you think of any other solution?

SUPPLEMENTARY READING CONTRACT

Reading Instructional Levels 11–16   *Nonfiction*

Name_____ Reading Class_____

Reading Level_____Regular Class_____Date_____

Title of Book_____

Author of Book_____# of pages_____

Publisher of Book_____Date of Publication_____

Please complete all the information above and answer all the questions below. You may use extra paper if you do not have enough room on this sheet.

———————————

Describe the topic of this book.

Tell why you wanted to read about this topic.

Tell some things you learned about this topic which you didn't know before.

SUPPLEMENTARY READING CONTRACT

Reading Instructional Levels 17–20   *Nonfiction*

Name_____   Reading Class_____

Reading Level_____Regular Class_____Date_____

Title of Book_____

Author of Book_____# of pages_____

Publisher of Book_____Date of Publication_____

Please complete all the information above and answer *all the questions* below. You may use extra paper if you do not have enough room on this sheet.

Describe the topic of this book.

What other books or magazine articles or films have you seen or read on this topic?

What would you like to know about this topic that you did not find in this book? List the names and authors of other books, articles, or films (use media center card catalog) which will tell you more about this topic.

three.

SUPPLEMENTARY READING CONTRACT

Reading Instructional Levels 17–20   *Fiction*

Name_____   Reading Class_____

Reading Level_____Regular Class_____Date_____

Title of Book_____

Author of Book_____# of pages_____

Publisher of Book_____Date of Publication_____

Please complete all the information above. Read the questions below and pick out *any three* which you wish to answer on the back of this sheet. You may use more paper if you need it.

———————

Authors write. Readers read. Authors write because they have something to say. Are they successful in getting their ideas across to their readers? Each reader is different. Each reader may react differently to the same book. When you read a book of fiction, what do you get out of it besides the story? Here are some questions to help you find out. Remember to answer only three.

1. How did you get involved in the story?
2. Explain how the people in the book were real like you or like other people you know.
3. Explain how this book made you think, how it stretched your imagination, how it presented a point of view new to you.
4. What in this book was really important to you?
5. Explain how this story could have taken place in a geographical location other than the one the author used.
6. Explain how this book could have taken place in an age or time in the past or future other than the time the author used.
7. Explain what you would have done if you had been in the same situation as the main character in the book.
8. Explain whether this book is about man against nature, man against machine, man against people, man against himself.

activities which will involve his class more deeply and completely in the communication arts. He wants the children to have literary, art and music experience all centered around this theme, because of its universality at all times and all places. He intends to bring out the different ways in which authors, artists, composers, poets, film makers, T.V. producers and even newsmen treat this same theme. He announces that as a year-end activity in language arts he would like to put on a festival of all the communication arts which will last six weeks and will feature a weekly happening. The first event will be a film on a subject similar to that of a book which the whole class has read together with a discussion comparing them following. The second happening will be a book panel on the three most popular books as voted by the class from a booklist on the theme. If possible a local author will be invited to participate. The third week a debate will be held to decide which recent T.V. show and film on courage was best. The fourth event will be an art show and poetry reading which will combine reproductions and original art by children and others, with poetry on courage located in the media center and written by children as a response to the works of art, books, films and T.V. programs. The fifth event will be a performance of all types of songs on valor and courage located by the class in the media center and prepared during music class. The sixth and final Grand Happening will be a performance which will summarize the total experience for an audience by:

Introducing the film about the book read in common and showing a small but key part of it as illustration

Introducing and dramatizing a key scene from each of the three favorite books

Showing some of the art and reproductions and reading live or on tape the poetry inspired by it

Performing some of the songs, explaining the meaning of each one if necessary

Writing a commentary to tie all the parts together.

The curtain raiser for this adventure in the communication arts is a book talk on some of the following books of which many titles are available in multiple paperback copies in the media center.

Buck, *The Big Wave*	Arnold, *A Kind of Secret Weapon*
Bishop, *Twenty and Ten*	Sperry, *Call It Courage*
Hinton, *The Outsiders*	Frank, *Diary of Anne Frank*

Bloch, *Aunt America*	Donovan, *I'll Get There. It Better Be*
Armstrong, *Sounder*	*Worth the Trip*
Graham, *South Town*	Sterling, *Mary Jane*
Day, *Landslide!*	Viereck, *The Summer I Was Lost*
Lee, *The Skating Rink*	Wojciekowska, *Shadow of a Bull*

As a common reading the media specialist suggests that the teacher read *The Big Wave* to the class. The film *The Wave,*[9] based on a Japanese folktale, is an excellent short film to use for a two-pronged comparison: (1) of the film with the book by Margaret Hodges,[10] and (2) of the folktale (on film) with a novel on the same subject—a tidal wave.

Committees are appointed to: (1) list suitable films and T.V. programs weekly, some of which are assigned as homework; (2) collect art reproductions and slides in the media center, including sculpture, stained glass, etc.; (3) locate poetry and copy it; (4) find songs and music to learn and play; (5) find news articles in magazines and newspapers to cut out and post.

Bulletin boards with these materials are prepared: the creative prose and poetry contrasting with the news items, the creative writing commenting on the original art work and reproductions. Limited space for display will make the children more selective as to what to hang. A discussion of what is best will develop judgment and taste.

The media specialist sees to it that the intercultural scope of the book talk is continued in the other areas by directing the children to poetry, music and art created by members of many of our minority groups, who had the courage to keep going in spite of heavy odds, as evidenced in Langston Hughes' poem *Mother To Son*.

GOAL IV: PRODUCTION OF MEDIA MATERIALS

Primary and Intermediate

Scattered through this chapter are examples of simple media materials produced by children and used by them for the presentation of a report to show what they have discovered and to share it with others. Sometimes the produced media materials are so attrac-

---

9. *The Wave, A Japanese Folktale,* Film Associates, 1968, 9 minutes, 16mm, color.

10. Margaret Hodges, *The Wave.* Adapted from Lafcadio Hearn's *Gleanings in Buddha-fields.* Illustrated by Blair Lent. Houghton Miffin, 1964.

tive and well done that they are added to the permanent media collection. It is rather arbitrary to say that certain production skills are primary and others intermediate. As soon as a child can operate a machine he can produce something with that machine. In order of ease of handling taping comes first, then copying with the opaque projector, making a simple transparency, photographing (instamatic), and film making. Once a child can handle these machines, the only limit is his imagination.

Tape Production

Take book-records. These are book talks by children on tape. Children on all levels may promote a book they have enjoyed by talking about it on tape. Book-records on one subject are spliced together to serve as reading motivation. There is no better motivation than a recommendation by another child, even if you don't know him. A visual extension of a book-record is its illustration with stick figures on the overhead, while playing the tape—marvelous for a large group.

The picture book read into tape with simple sound effects if suitable or with music background softly recorded—the producer finds his own music to suit the story—can be used as a small group independent reading experience by beginning readers. They must listen carefully and follow the spoken word on the page to turn it at the right moment. They must watch for clues. Many excellent modern picture books now come in paperback; purchasing them in multiple copies is not too great a strain on the budget. Having children read them into tape is so much better than buying them in hard covers read by adults, and much cheaper too!

Film or Acetate Strips

Making your own "transtrip" is a very satisfying way of giving a presentation. A transtrip is a flimstrip on 8½x11 acetate transparencies, drawn by hand and colored with indelible markers, fastened together by plastic hinges. Captions are used or put on tape and for storage the transtrip is folded accordion fashion and put in a folder. Clear filmstrip is now available to draw on with just about anything that writes. It is good for children who have the kind of control over their fingers that permits them to draw on a small surface.

Photography and Slides

Photography can be used by children most effectively, even when they are quite young. When the curriculum includes a social studies unit for third-year students on the local community as a geographic, economic and governmental unit, photography with instamatic cameras is a marvelous reporting tool. In some areas the school neighborhood includes something of everything that can be found in the community at large. Garden apartments are next door to small office buildings. There is a factory, a small park, a major highway, a shopping plaza, with a bank, a railroad crossing, a firehouse, garage and post office; two churches of different denominations; architectural examples ranging from late colonial through Victorian to modern; even an old farm and some rural slums. All these rich resources within walking distance and without having to cross the highway! Ideal to take children in small groups to take slides. Arranging the finished slides by subjects and taping notes as commentary is a great learning experience. The show will be a permanent asset to the resources on the local community.

Films

Then there is film making. The most automatic movie camera is the best, if children are to use it. It should have a slow-motion device which also permits the taking of single exposures for animation. Many super 8 cameras now come with a cassette tape recorder, synchronized by cables with the camera. With this kind of equipment it is possible to make instructional and creative films. The gym teacher who teaches acrobatics and equipment skills can take films of her best students in fast and slow motion to be used for teaching. A film-making club is a good way to teach a small group of children how to develop an idea into a film. They become very observant about details, when films are shown without sound. They are shown how to make a storyboard for their film. When they have plotted it sequentially, they have to anticipate problems they may have to solve in the actual filming. They make their films one at the time in the A-V room of the media center, or outdoors as the case may be. The following year they become the teachers of another group of children who want to make a film.

Multi-media Productions

Giving a multi-media show is a fine way of showing an audience that what was learned, truly became part of you. When fifth- and sixth-year students became fascinated with African music, sculpture and jewelry, this is what happened. The media center had an excellent set of sound filmstrips by Warren Schloat Productions, which the children located through the card catalog. One of the boys, an enthusiastic drummer, was hooked by the music, drums and instruments on the part called *Africa, Musical Instruments, Textiles, Jewelry* and *Architecture*. When the girls saw a lot of boys listening and looking, they wanted to see it too. They fell for the jewelry and textiles, and took the set out to show to the art teacher, who capitalized on their interest by teaching pattern and motif, based on African designs. The children began to examine fabrics people wore; some even went to the local fabric shop and brought back small pieces of fabrics based on African motifs. They printed their own designs on old sheets to make fabrics. They made jewelry, flat collars woven on wire of tiny love beads, and earhoops (worn over the ear) of large clay beads of self-hardening clay, painted in brilliant colors. The art teacher used the other sound filmstrip in the set: *African Art and Culture*. The classroom committee that was studying African animals created their own clay sculptures of them. An *Art on Tour* exhibit on Africian art and crafts came at this time and stayed in the media center for two weeks. (The teacher had timed his unit to coincide with this exhibit by consulting the *Art on Tour* schedule of exhibits for the year in the media center.) The media specialist gave an introduction to African folktales, just a few days—and this was serendipity—before a black folklorist from New York, sponsored by the New York State Council of the Arts and the school district, came to the school for story-telling sessions on all levels.

She was dressed in African fashion, with a jelle´ (wrap around turban) on her head, bedecked with jewelry, much like what the children were working on. There was an instant bond and rapport much different from the relationship she established with other groups. As soon as she left the children came to borrow all the African folktales that were left. Additional materials were ordered from the district's Title II Interlibrary Loan Collection (a library of about 10,000 volumes and other media established with Title II funds).

A folktale committee memorized three folktales and wanted to go around the school to tell them. The teacher then suggested that instead of repeating what already had been done, the class put on a multi-media show to let others share their experiences. The three folktales took center stage, in front of a large movie screen which hangs far enough back so that the action can take place in front of it. Costumes for the people in the stories were made with the fabrics the children had printed. They wore the jewelry they had made. The animals wore a very simple headgear (e.g. the elephant just had two large grey cardboard ears) and acted their part by the way they moved. Instead of painted flats, jungle and village scenes were painted with magic marker on acetate sheets, for projection with the overhead projector, and instantly changed as needed. Appropriate jungle sounds were taped in advance and played at the right moments.

The folktales were introduced by an African village story teller, preceded and followed by a drum ensemble of three natives. Authentic African songs, sung in African languages, found in the media center on Folkways records, were sung by the villagers as they waited for the next story to begin. They were accompanied by rhythm instruments. (All music was prepared and rehearsed in music class.)

The authenticity lent a great deal of excitement to this multimedia production. The projected backdrops were particularly suggestive of the setting sun and the hot brilliance of the landscape because of their luminosity. This viewer was there, sitting on the village square, as the hot sun was setting and wild animal eyes were peering through the jungle growth behind the native huts.

This chapter is just a sampler. Its limitations prevent the inclusion of methods used to incorporate other skills and experiences in the media curriculum and the school curriculum. More ideas and materials may be found in Chapter 7. Many variations are possible, depending on facilities, the strength and depth of the media collection, and the individual strengths of teachers and media specialists. By building from areas of strength and working at first with teachers willing to try new approaches, the media world will enliven the curriculum, give it a third dimension and thereby make it viable for today's children.

4

Involving Teachers
in the Media Center

TEACHERS AND THE MEDIA CENTER

No amount of equipment, physical design, or software makes a media center. Even a great media specialist does not a media center make. Teachers can make a media center work. The media center works to the extent that teachers participate with their children in the multi-faceted opportunities offered through the media center. A knowledgeable school administration and a skilled media specialist will help launch the media concept off the ground. It will help in planning the program, doing the ordering, and organizing the schedule to have these two people. But beyond these two necessary people participation depends upon teachers and their children.

Strategies must be employed to involve the teaching staff in continued utilization of the media center for it to become an integral part of the regular school program. Ideally each teacher must plan her weekly program to include individual and small group, as well as class, plans for media center utilization. When each teacher plans this way, when it becomes a normal part of her teaching routine, then you have a media center which is a viable and exciting operational plant. At this point too, teachers begin to make such demands upon the media center that the specialist will be hard put to offer all the services required. And this, of course, is the goal of the media center: to broaden, enrich, and titillate the learning experiences of each child; to make it a natural part of the total school environment of the child. A media center is multi media, multi sense, multi experience. It must be used this way.

INTERESTED TEACHERS

Let us assume that we have the interest and enthusiasm for a media center program. Let us assume a gung ho administration and a librarian ready to make the transition to media specialist. They have a vision, an idea, a thought, and they are ready to proceed. It is at this point that teacher involvement becomes crucial. Teachers who become involved at this point will be the teachers who will use the media center. Initial involvement can be accomplished through invitation if there has been no expressed interest on the part of certain teachers. Usually there is a group of teachers in a school building who are ready for the new and exciting. It is these teachers whom administration must embrace. Discussions on an informal level with these teachers about the beginnings of a media program and what it can offer are pursued. The group can then move to more formalized group discussions with specific short-range topics. The most fruitful topic to start might well be teacher expectations from the media program. This topic permits the exploration of many media concepts. Administration and the media specialist suggest some of the many things they envision from the media program. The group has now compiled a list of many suggestions for the media program in its initial stages. It is imperative that teacher suggestions which come from this initial group of teachers be heeded and heeded carefully, even if they do not coincide with the plans of the media specialist or administration. These suggestions refined and clarified can form the nucleus for the first programs offered to the teachers when the plan becomes operational.

We do not suggest in-service courses or other techniques for initial involvement in the media center before the program becomes operational. We have found that in-service courses or workshops work best after a plan is in operation and teachers can relate the course offerings to their practical day-to-day problems in the classroom.

If the initial discussions with the teachers are not particularly creative or visionary, we would not be concerned. Initial programs should be offered in the media center which fulfill teachers' original requests from the program. One might add to the program one or two administration or media specialist contributions, but that is all. We would start the program with the simplest of operational plans. They have the most chance for teacher involvement and, more importantly, for teacher support. Let us give some examples.

TEACHER SUGGESTIONS

A teacher suggests that she would like some help from the media specialist in having children do research for their social studies units. Her suggestion is rather vague. The discussions at this point might well be broadened. The initiating media team (administration and media specialist) could expand on this thought. They might very easily explain in broad outline the many skills a child requires in order to do a "piece of research." As the discussion continues, the media specialist might show how the many sequential skills the children need to master could be outlined. Further the media specialist and the teacher might well plan together for the children in this one class to learn these skills in sequential order as they work on a particular series of units of study in the social studies. Certain skills would be undertaken by the media specialist through the media center program and followed up in the classroom. Other skills might be initiated in the classroom by the classroom teacher with the media specialist offering resources only. This interrelated kind of operation is the soul of the media center program. Once a program of this sort is operated with one teacher successfully, it becomes infectious. Other teachers can see that their work with children can be enhanced and enriched through these shared experiences. After some time, this teacher's experience with the media program becomes a model for other similar operations. Meeting with other teachers of the same grade level or group might now be encouraged to endorse further utilization of the model. You have now set up the embryo of Goal Two (the utilization of media materials) plans for one group of teachers. The planning can now be worked into the open schedule program and become an operational part of the weekly routine.

BUILD GRADUALLY

The pattern we suggest is obvious. Work from an individual teacher to a small group of teachers and, finally, to all the teachers, until certain patterns become routine in the entire school with only teachers new to the school needing formal orientation. We recommend this pattern. We feel slower but greater success can be achieved than by attempting to initiate a program throughout the entire school at one time. There really is no way to predict how long these patterns take to become routine since every situation is so totally different. But with patient maneuvering from one-teacher involvement to group involvement, larger and larger strategies can be encompassed in the regular planning for the media center program.

Let's look at another example. A teacher in your initial group of teacher leaders might well suggest that she would like to work on Haiku with her sixth-year children when they study the Far East, but she never had the time or the materials for pursuing this interest. Again this interest can be turned to good use. The media specialist could offer his services as a resource person on a Haiku unit. The classroom teacher could teach the Haiku form as a series of lessons in the classroom, while the media specialist could collect and distribute books on Haiku poetry, reprints of Japanese paintings which so often express Haiku pictorially, recordings of Japanese music, and showings of Japanese films. Children might be sent to the media center during the poetry unit for this resource material and learn to share it with the class. This would be a breakthrough in the accomplishment of Goal Three (appreciation of media material). Other teachers might have art interests which they might wish to share with their classes, and will recognize that the media center can provide resources far beyond the classroom to broaden the particular art experience they wish to develop. It might work the other way around. The media specialist, apprised of the areas of study in each class, might make suggestions to particular teachers around particular areas of study they are pursuing with their classes. The media specialist could loan to the teacher much background material for the unit of study. He might offer a collection of native folk music and a collection of African realia (borrowed) to a group of teachers working on Africa in social studies. Thus from both ends—teacher to media specialist, media specialist to teacher—suggestions for enriching units of study can be set up and subsequently propagandized for further teacher involvement in like pursuits.

Once a teacher uses the resources of the media center for an area of curriculum work, she is ready to think media center when she plans still further curriculum work.

The initial group discussions lead to another avenue. One teacher suggested she is bored with the uncreative, pedestrian way her children present their research reports to their classmates. Here, of course, is the opening of the door to exploration of Goal Four (the production of media materials). This teacher wants other suggestions for presentations, other methods, other techniques. This area may indeed not be her strength. The media specialist can offer to show this teacher and her class other methods for media production in her program and set up a working arrangement for them. The skills might well be taught to the class by the media specialist, but the creation of the media themselves would be part of the classroom curriculum.

WORKSHOPS

Here, it would be quite easy to talk in terms of workshops. We are firm believers in short-term workshops given on a few afternoons which fulfill a specific felt need at a specific time. In-service courses are generally given by districts for long periods of time. What we are talking about are short-range workshops with very specific and precise goals—a workshop showing interested teachers how to make transparencies for overhead projectors; a workshop showing teachers how to make single-loop 8mm films; a workshop showing teachers how to cut a stencil. These are the kinds of experiences that reap rich harvests for schools. They are practical, have precise goals, and teachers can usually find a use for the experience in their classrooms once they have mastered the technique.

We have tried to give examples which show how the initial experiences with the initial group of interested teacher leaders can be utilized to build and broaden a media center program. Each idea can be expanded, once a model is established, to include more curriculum areas and more teachers. We believe the program must be started with the interested teachers and then skillfully made to grow larger and more detailed and more specific until such point in time that all teachers are participating in varying degrees in the media center program. The final step is use by all teachers for the accomplishment of all four instructional goals.

CLUSTER MEETINGS

Beyond the actual initial point in the program other strategies might well be utilized to broaden teacher involvement in the media program. One of the most effective we elect to call cluster meetings. They may go by such time-honored names as grade level meetings, team meetings, or group meetings. Whatever their name, the exchange of ideas for curriculum growth and change can only come through teacher involvement, teacher awareness, and teacher interest. Weekly scheduled cluster meetings with administration and the media specialist present afford this opportunity as no other strategy we know. Somehow we have found that the total faculty meeting is not so productive a medium. The smaller group meeting is the arena where small concerns, problems, and ideas can best be explored. It is here that they can be openly and freely discussed. Although weekly cluster meetings will have many items on their agenda—discipline problems, learning problems, parental problems—the hidden agenda can always be movement toward a more viable and creative media center program. If administration is alert to direct tie-ins between so-called classroom curriculum and the media center, suggestions can often be given which will bring the media specialist into the picture. Once the media specialist's contributions to particular problems become visible, more and more involvement can be planned. The media program must, in a way, create a role for itself whenever the opportunity exists.

For example, if a group of intermediate teachers complains at a cluster meeting that there is not enough material available for the study of early America with six classes pursuing the study at the same time, some solutions might be offered. It might be possible to stagger the study of early America so that all classes are not studying this topic at the same time. The media specialist could arrange for all materials to be centralized in the media center and each class pursue their studies at a different time in the school year. Better still the media specialist might plan for everyone to study the unit at the same time by organizing certain portions of the study for large group instruction with specific relevant topics of study for each separate class. In other words, curriculum areas can be utilized as the avenue to further involvement and planning between teachers and the media specialist. Once again, if a plan of this sort works the first time around, teachers will think in terms of using the media specialist in their future unit plans. Hopefully, in time all units of study could be discussed and planned in advance with the media specialist.

The idea is to get each teacher involved in the media program through some area of interest or concern which she has. Eventually these many different kinds of plans, with their different goals and objectives, can be planned and organized in an intricate open schedule plan as discussed in Chapter 3. One proceeds step by step. There should be no particular order to the establishment of the program. The order should follow naturally and normally the suggestions by classroom teachers at meetings formal and informal and should fulfill their needs as they see them initially. More sophisticated and elaborate media center programs will evolve in time. Eventually a total program and only a total program will meet the teachers' requirements of the media center. Although one teacher may have been brought into the media center through Haiku poetry, she will remain long after when she sees the results and when she observes what others are doing in terms of research skills for social studies, production of tapes for speeches, and the endless other experiences being tried and offered by other teachers through the media specialist.

Cluster meetings become the arena for discussing successful implementation of various media center involvements. The programs need publicity. Teachers must be encouraged to talk about their programs in the media center. The spirit becomes infectious. The media center is viewed as a helping arm. It can make for every teacher a more exciting day. It can enlarge her own plans and her own thinking. Cluster meetings are an indispensable aid for curriculum growth and change. They should be built into each school's weekly plans. Limit full faculty meetings to once a month if need be, but don't forego any opportunity to hold cluster meetings on a weekly basis.

VISITATIONS

There are other procedures which can help in building teacher involvement in the media program. One time-honored and effective method is visitation. Teacher visits to other schools which have successful programs in operation are often quite helpful. Visiting teachers can see how children and teachers become involved in a media center, and return to home base quite enthusiastic about their own future involvement.

CENTRAL STORAGE

Within one's own school other techniques should be encouraged. One is quite simple. Store almost all media and material for adults and children in a centralized location. The tendency would be, in other words, to keep as little material as possible on loan in classrooms. In a way teachers and children would be forced to come to the media center to follow their studies. There would not be enough information, in print even, kept in the classroom to conduct a realistic piece of research. Exposure to the media center is important. This is an indirect way to get both teachers and children to the media center for material. Once there, they explore, find other materials and begin to recognize the importance of the media center.

THE RELUCTANT TEACHER

One word of caution here. Teacher resistance is a fact of life. Most schools will have some teachers on staff who will offer passive or active resistance to a media program at its inception. This type of resistance is normal and natural and need not be feared. The feelings of the teacher who holds back from participation in the media program should be respected. Further, she should even be allowed to keep her own treasure of classroom books intact in her room. One essential to the success of the long-term media program is acceptance by teachers at their own moment of comfort. The teacher who needs to hold onto her own classroom library would be permitted to do so without any fear of disapproval by the administration. In fact, the clever media specialist will build a better classroom library for this teacher. The better library is a first step showing the classroom teacher that the media specialist can serve as a resource person.

The few teachers on staff who will prefer this method of operation do exist. They will continue to exist for a time. After a while, a few years even, the action throughout the rest of the school, the stimulation of the program itself will draw in the most reluctant. There will come a moment when this teacher will reach out and the media specialist will begin to draw this teacher and this class into the media program.

Two factors are always working to help this teacher accept the media program and release her own class-library program: first, the other teachers who are actively involved in the media program and who talk about it and share their results; second, the children in this teacher's class who may have media experiences from another class which they recall fondly or children who watch other children operate and want a "piece of the action" too. Thus other teachers and the children in the class become media allies. We stress, therefore, that direct or indirect pressure from administration need not be applied to these few hesitant individuals. Time and patience will make converts of them.

MEDIA AND CURRICULUM PLANS

Still another but more complicated approach to teacher involvement in the utilization of the media center can be planned. Particular curriculum plans can be made which require media center use. For example, all teachers teach reading in the elementary school. They teach certain specific skills, but along with this teaching generally also comes some plan for reading for pleasure, for enrichment—supplementary reading, if you will. Suppose this area of reading became more formalized. Let's say that for every level a child masters in reading skills he is also expected to read a minimum of one book "on his own." Just such an arrangement has been worked out in our school. (See Reading Contracts, pages 66-72). Now every child must come to the media center on his own to select with the careful help of the media specialist a book to read in order to fulfill his "Reading Contract." In this method all children are given further and purposeful exposure to the media center with their teacher's full involvement and the help of the media specialist. The media specialist helps in the book selection. The teacher helps in the contract selection and reads the completed contract.

In time all throughout the school different media center programs will be in operation. From that one moves to more definitive plans for groups of teachers in a specific area, for example, a science unit on space for sixth-year children. From this comes further exposition and a move toward the incorporation of open schedule plans for all intermediate classes and, finally, for the entire school. One can pursue this line of development for each of the four goals outlined in Chapter 3, till they are an integral part of the total school program for all classes. Don't try to institute the total master plan for starters. Let the teachers' suggestions and needs lead to the utilization of the media center as they originally see the media center fulfilling their needs. Move from one individual's needs to one group's needs. Move finally from one group's needs to the total school's needs. It is a safer and more efficient plan of operation. It will produce success more slowly, but it will produce. Large, elaborate plans for everyone have built in traps. Often the total media program can be lost in the process and, of course, this should be avoided at all costs.

TEACHER CONSULTATIONS WITH THE MEDIA SPECIALIST

One final word. If you remember, in Chapter 3 we talked about one sixth of the media specialist's time being reserved for many activities other than meeting with children. Part of this time, as we have demonstrated throughout this chapter, must be utilized by the media specialist in meeting with teachers. The media specialist must meet with teachers on an individual or small group basis. He must

5

Techniques and Activities for Implementing Media Instructional Goal One: Children Learn to Locate Media Material

FACULTY INVOLVEMENT IS THE KEY

Additional units and materials to involve children and faculty in media and media skills is the essence of this chapter. Many of these materials are in puzzle form or take the shape of a contest. Not all are related to units of study but may be used separately, whenever opportune. Most materials found here may be fitted into units of study at the most teachable moment. This teachable moment is on most occasions carefully planned by the teacher and media specialist together.

It is of course an advantage to teach media skills sequentially but it is not absolutely necessary, because the same skills will be taught in different ways and depth and context, several times in a child's elementary school life. Although the activities and materials which follow are prefaced by the goals to which they pertain, it must always be kept in mind that none of these four goals can be cleanly separated from the others, as they are all interrelated. They work together to build the total involvement with media one expects to achieve through a media center program.

EMPHASIS ON PRINTED MATERIALS

In Chapter 3 a unit on the primary level described Goal I—

Locating Media Materials. With second and third year children a unit in locating materials independently through use of the card catalog and reading lists is planned with heavy emphasis on books. It is called *Book Read-in* and in six meetings the skills outlined below are covered. These skills are the foundation on which Goal II—*The Utilization of Media*—is built. During each lesson, time is spent introducing each class group to key books and authors on reading lists (BOOK BEE) by means of the most suitable media (pages 91-95).

Lesson I: Locating of fiction by author's last name on bookshelves

Shelving of fiction by first three letters of author's last name (prepared cards are used for this activity)

Reviewing of title page information

Developing library vocabulary from these activities to be added to reading vocabulary of the class

Lesson II: Fiction BOOK BEES distributed

Choosing a book from the list to locate on the shelves

Examining the book for readability and enjoyment

Utilizing title page information to complete a simple programmed book report (FICTION BOOK BUZZ) in class (page 97)

Lesson III: Fiction BOOK GUESS-IN sheets distributed

Formulating a riddle about the content of a fiction book

Including a key word as a clue (page 98)

Lesson IV: The Dewey Decimal System arrangement of nonfiction explained

Locating a nonfiction book by call number (prepared cards are used for this activity)

Borrowing a nonfiction book

Lesson V: FACT BOOK BUZZ sheets are distributed

Examination of the parts of nonfiction books

Explanation of FACT BOOK BUZZ sheets and how to complete them

Utilizing the parts of a nonfiction book to complete FACT BOOK BUZZES in class (page 96)

Lesson VI: Location of a subject, fiction or nonfiction, in the card catalog (prepared cards are used for this activity)

Location of the book on the shelves after writing down of call number and title, or author letters and title.

BOOK READ-IN   No. 1   ELMWOOD MEDIA CENTER

Name_____ Class_____

BOOK BEE

Authors	Titles
Anderson, C. W.	Blaze and the Gypsies
Anderson, C. W.	Blaze and the Lost Quarry
Anderson, C. W.	Blaze and the Forest Fire
Beim, Jerrold	Two Is a Team
Beim, Jerrold	Thin Ice
*Benchley, Nathaniel	Oscar Otter
Brenner, Barbara	Beef Stew
Bright, Robert	Georgie
Brown, M. W.	Goodnight Moon
Carrick, Carol	The Old Barn
Colman, Hila	Peter's Brownstone House
*Elkin, Benjamin	The Big Jump and Other Stories
Floethe, L. L.	The Cowboy On the Ranch
*Friskey, Margaret	Indian Two Feet and His Horse
*Hoff, Carol	The Four Friends
*Holland, Marion	A Big Ball of String
Keats, E. J.	Peter's Chair
*LeSieg, Theo	Ten Apples Up On Top!
*Lexau, J. M.	The Homework Caper
Lexau, Joan	Olaf Reads
*McClintock, Mike	What Have I Got?
Moore, Lilian	The Magic Spectacles
Olds, H. D.	Kate Can Skate

*starred books are easier than the others

BOOK READ-IN   No. 2   ELMWOOD MEDIA CENTER

Name_____ Class_____

BOOK BEE

Authors	Titles
Rey, Margaret	Curious George Goes to the Hospital
Wahl, Jan	Cabbage Moon
*Bridwell, Norman	The Witch Next Door
Graham, M. S.	Be Nice to Spiders
*Hillert, Margaret	The Little Runaway
Kinney, Jean	What Does the Tide Do?
*Simon, Norma	What Do I Say?
Surany, Anico	The Covered Bridge
Tresselt, Alvin	The World In the Candy Egg
Alexander, Anne	Noise In the Night
Anderson, C. W.	Blaze and Thunderbolt
Anderson, C. W.	Blaze Finds the Trail
Ardizzone, Edward	Little Tim and the Brave Sea Captain
*Averill, Esther	The Fire Cat
*Baker, Betty	Little Runner of the Longhouse
Beim, Jerrold	The Smallest Boy in the Class
*Benchley, Nathaniel	Red Fox and His Canoe
*Berenstein, Stanley	Bear's Vacation
*Kessler, Leonard	Kick, Pass and Run
*Bonsall, Crosby	The Case of the Hungry Stranger
*Brenner, Barbara	The Five Pennies
Brown, M. W.	The Dead Bird
Kumin, M. W.	A Winter Friend

---

*starred books are easier to read than the others

BOOK READ-IN   No. 3   ELMWOOD MEDIA CENTER

Name_____ Class_____

BOOK BEE

Authors	*Titles*
Hoban, Russell	Bedtime for Frances
McLeod, Emilie	One Snail and Me
Flack, Marjorie	The Story About Ping
Burton, V. L.	Little House
Brunhoff, Jean de	The Story of Babar
Rey, H. A.	Curious George
Ungerer, Tomi	Crictor
Ungerer, Tomi	The Three Robbers
Caudill, Rebecca	The Best Loved Doll
Anderson, C. W.	Billy and Blaze
Anderson, C. W.	Blaze and the Mountain Lion
Titus, Eve	Anatole
Titus, Eve	Anatole and the Robot
Slobodkina, Esphyr	Caps for Sale
Zion, Gene	Harry the Dirty Dog
Merrill, Jean	Tell About the Cowbarn, Daddy
Keats, Ezra	Jennie's Hat
Tresselt, Alvin	The Mitten
Freeman, Don	Come Again, Pelican
Kumin, M. W.	Eggs of Things
Ets, M. H.	Bad Boy, Good Boy
Burton, V. L.	Mike Mulligan and His Steam Shovel
Waber, Bernard	Just Like Abraham Lincoln

BOOK READ-IN   No. 4   ELMWOOD MEDIA CENTER

Name_____ Class_____

BOOK BEE

Authors	*Titles*
Felt, Sue	Rosa-Too-Little
Udry, J. M.	What Mary Jo Shared
Udry, J. M.	A Tree Is Nice
Bemelmans, Ludwig	Madeline's Rescue
Freeman, Don	Corduroy
Hader, Bertha	Snow In the City
McCloskey, Robert	Make Way For Ducklings
DuBois, W. P.	Otto At Sea
DuBois, W. P.	Otto In Africa
DuBois, W. P.	Bear Party
Selden, George	Sparrow Socks
Zolotow, Charlotte	Big Sister, Little Sister
Zion, Gene	The Summer Snowman
Zion, Gene	The Plant Sitter
Zion, Gene	No Roses for Harry!
Lionni, Leo	Tico and the Golden Wings
Leaf, Munro	The Story of Ferdinand
Rose, Carl	The Crazy Zoo That Dudley Drew
Sendak, Maurice	Where the Wild Things Are
Shortall, Leonard	Ben On the Ski Trail
Shortall, Leonard	Danny On the Lookout
Shortall, Leonard	Sam's First Fish
Thayer, Jane	The Puppy Who Wanted a Boy
Thayer, Jane	The Outside Cat

BOOK READ-IN   No. 5   ELMWOOD MEDIA CENTER

Name_____ Class_____

BOOK BEE

Author	*Titles*
Charlip, Remy	Fortunately
Cleary, Beverly	The Real Hole
Cole, William	Frances Face-Maker
Collier, Ethel	I Know a Farm
DeLage, Ida	The Farmer and the Witch
DuBois, W. P.	Bear Party
Duvoisin, Roger	Petunia Takes a Trip
*Eastman, P. D.	Are You My Mother?
Ets, M. H.	Gilberto and the Wind
Fatio, Louise	The Happy Lion
*Flack, Marjorie	Ask Mr. Bear
*Fox, C. P.	Come To the Circus
*Tensen, R. M.	Come To the Zoo
Gramatky, Hardie	Hercules
Swift, Hildegarde	The Little Red Lighthouse
*Guilfoile, Elizabeth	Nobody Listens to Andrew
*Heilbroner, Joan	The Happy Birthday Present
Hoff, Syd	Lengthy
Holl, Adelaide	The Rain Puddle
Holt, Margaret	David McCheever's 29 Dogs
Hurd, E. T.	Johnny Lion's Book
*Kessler, Ethel	Do Baby Bears Sit In Chairs?
*Platt, Kin	Big Max

*starred books are easier to read than the others.

BOOK READ-IN   ELMWOOD MEDIA CENTER

Name_____Class_____

FACT BOOK BUZZ

Author:_____
          first name   last name

Title:_____

(check (✓) what is true for your book)
This book: _____ has much information
           _____ is interesting all the way
           _____ has interesting parts
           _____ is not interesting

This book: _____ has a table of contents
           _____ has an index
           _____ has pictures with captions to explain them
           _____ is up-to-date (less than 5 years old)

Choose one new fact you learned from this book:
_____

Choose one new word you learned from this book:
1._____, _____
          word   meaning

BOOK READ-IN   ELMWOOD MEDIA CENTER

Name_____ Class_____

FICTION BOOK BUZZ

Author:_____

      first name   last name

Title:_____

This story is (underline one):   easy   hard   very hard.

Here are some words in this story that were hard for me:

_____

_____

_____

The most important person, animal or thing in this story is:

_____

_____

What happens to him (or it)?

_____

_____

_____

_____

BOOK READ-IN   ELMWOOD MEDIA CENTER

Name_____ Class_____

BOOK GUESS-IN

Make up a riddle about a book you have just read. Put in some clues so that someone who has not read it can find it in the Subject Catalog. Make it very short. Have a quiz. As you read more books, write more riddles.

Example:
Author:__*Brunhoff*____ Title:__*The Story of Babar*
         last name

I am an elephant. An old lady is my best friend. Who am I?

1. Author:_____ Title:_____
          last name

_____

_____

_____

2. Author:_____ Title:_____
          last name

_____

_____

_____

3. Author:_____ Title:_____
          last name

_____

_____

_____

CLASSROOM IMPLEMENTATION

Many classroom follow-up activities can be planned from this skills unit. In his conference with the classroom teachers the media specialist asks that the main concept of the unit—*The Alphabet and Numbers as an Organizational Tool*—be utilized and emphasized in the classroom whenever possible. Schemes and application are left to individual teachers to work out, unless they ask for ideas. A few interesting practical applications follow:

When the area was swept by the tail end of a hurricane, one teacher had the children find out what the names of previous hurricanes were in previous years. In their first brush with the *World Almanac* in the media center, they discovered that all hurricanes are named after girls and that they are named in alphabetical order, as they occur.

Another teacher sent a team of four children around the school to observe and report back on how the alphabet and number system is used to organize the school. They found that classrooms have letters and are grouped into four clusters, named alpha, beta, gamma and delta. When they reported back they were informed that the cluster names are the first four letters of the Greek alphabet. They also noticed that the rooms are numbered, with downstairs numbers in the 100's and upstairs numbers in the 200's. In the office they found the rolldex pupil file, and many filing cabinets with labels from A–Z.

In another classroom the teacher decided that this was a good opportunity for dictionary work. She reads to her class every day, usually a chapter of a book. Each day she printed on small cards the more difficult words in the next day's chapter. If necessary she put them in context. The cards were placed in a box on her desk, labeled: Mystery Words. She numbered the cards sequentially as they occurred in the chapter. On an acetate sheet she listed the numbers in order. As an independent activity the children looked up the words and each child was allowed to write the meaning on the acetate, after the corresponding number. Each child also copied his word in his word book with the meaning. What a surprise when those words turned up in the next day's chapter and the meaning was right there for everyone to see on the overhead!

A once-a-week Book Guess was held in another classroom when

each child had made up enough book riddles to stump the class. The best riddles were lettered on colored oaktag, illustrated and hung around the story area of the media center.

EMPHASIS ON NON-PRINT MATERIALS AS INFORMATION SOURCES

On the intermediate level, a unit on MEDIA CENTER ORGANIZATION in depth emphasizes A-V materials as sources of information.

Lesson I: Subject: ORGANIZATION OF THE MEDIA CENTER

Large group meetings in auditorium with about 150 intermediate students including all new intermediate students.

Materials and Equipment—overhead projector, transparencies of vocabulary puzzle, map and programmed A-V report sheets; film on conventional library organization

Skills: Library vocabulary
             Map reading
             Following instructions
             Programmed reporting
             Handling of A-V equipment.

The media specialist shows a film on general library organization and presents the group with the differences between conventional libraries and media centers.

FOLLOW-UP ACTIVITIES IN PUZZLE AND PROGRAMMED FORM

On the overhead he shows transparencies of the follow-up activities, briefly explaining each one, explaining the procedure of doing them in the next four weeks, when the children will be scheduled in to the media center by their teachers to complete the puzzles and worksheets which follow each lesson, and are handed out to the teachers.

Lesson I, No. 1   ELMWOOD MEDIA CENTER

VOCABULARY PUZZLE   Name_____Class_____

It is your job to find the right words by filling in the blanks with letters and uncoding the other words. All words are library vocabulary and you will find them all on the signs posted around the library. To get credit for this activity all words must be correctly spelled. Quietly walk around the library, without talking, while you are solving these puzzles. In many cases the rhyme in the verses will give you a clue. (Answers to all puzzles, quizzes and games are in the Appendix)

1. A _ _ _i _ _ _ _ _ _ _
   Is methodical
   It arrives on the dot
   After a certain period.

2. For quick information
   Your first line of defense
   Should always be a book
   Of _ _ _ _ _ _ _ _ _ r (spelled backwards)

3. Want to know the meaning of a word?
   Even one you've never before heard?
   Why don't you try your hand
   At the _ _ _ _ _ _ _ _ _ _ stand?

4. The next 4 words are in the same cipher.
   Be a Sherlock Holmes and decipher them!
   We have a lot of 16 1 13 16 8 12 5 20 19
   In our 9 14 6 15 18 13 1 20 9 15 14   6 9 12 5.

5. If books of 6 9 3 20 9 15 14 are your cup of tea,
   Find them arranged by author from A—Z.

6. In the itcurepay ilefay we have stored
   Goodies for your teacher's bulletin board.

7. A _ _ _ _ _ _ _ _ _ is the true story
   Of someone's life;
   His ups and downs,
   His triumphs and strife.

Lesson I, No. 1

8. Don't press your luck
   Return your books on time
   And put them on the _ _ _ _ _ _ _ _ _.

9. There are pictures of person, beast and place
   In the stu dyprin tand pos terca se.

10. In the _ _ _ _ _ _ _ _ _ _ o _
    Do take a look
    See if you can find
    An interesting book.

11. Even more fun
    Than you find in a barrel
    Is viewing and listening
    In a study _ _ _ _ _ _.

12. The only books
    You can't have for yourselves,
    Are those displayed
    On the _ _ _ _ 1 _ _ shelves.

13. Everyone is able
    To sign his book card
    At a table.
    Then at the
    C _ _ _ _ _ _ _ d _ _ _
    He does the rest
    In A B C order
    It's filed
    In the c _ _ _ s _ _ _ _ _ .

14. If you like to read for information
    The n _ _ _ _ _ _ _ _ n shelves
    Should be your destination.

15. Be a jockey
    Without taking a risk
    Of being thrown,
    Just ride a _ _ _ c.

Lesson I, No. 2   ELMWOOD MEDIA CENTER

FILMSTRIP REPORT   Name _____Class _____

Follow instructions exactly and carefully!

Move quietly and do not talk except to ask for help and then only in a whisper.

1. Select only 1 filmstrip from the card catalog (red banded cards are filmstrip cards).
2. Write down the call number (on card at left) and the title on a slip of paper.
3. Ask the media aide (at the CHARGING DESK) to show you where to find it.
4. Take it to the CARREL marked PREVIEWERS.
5. Sit down and turn on the light switch; if light does not go on, check if previewer and carrel are plugged in.
6. Take filmstrip from can and replace lid; push can to back of carrel to make sure it does not fall down.
7. Find that end of filmstrip which says *start* or *focus* and insert it, right side up, in the rear slot of the machine.
8. Turn knob at right slowly, until the title of the filmstrip shows in the window. (title frame) (Each picture of a filmstrip is called a FRAME.)
9. Center the title frame in the window and focus the picture. (Black knob) Push silver knob in and turn to center the picture. Try to perform all these tasks by yourself. If you have trouble ask for help from the media aide or media specialist.
10. Now write down the title of the filmstrip: _____

_____

11. Turn the silver knob (down) to move to the next frame.
12. View the whole filmstrip and silently read the text in each frame.
13. When you are completely finished and *not sooner,* answer these questions:

    a. What is the main subject of the filmstrip you just saw?

_____

Lesson I, No. 2

b. Why did you choose a filmstrip on this subject?

_____

c. Would you recommend this filmstrip to your teacher for use with your class sometime this year when you are learning about this subject?

_____

d. Write down something new you learned from this filmstrip.

_____

_____

14. When you have finished *d.*, carefully remove the filmstrip from the machine.
15. Roll it up, starting at the end, so that the beginning is on the outside of the roll; pull it tight.
16. Replace the filmstrip in the can, put on the lid and return it to one of the wooden trays marked *Filmstrip Return,* on top of the filmstrip cabinets.

    P.S. To prevent mixing up of lids, you may take only 1 filmstrip at a time for viewing.

Lesson I, No. 3   ELMWOOD MEDIA CENTER

DISC REPORT   Name _____ Class _____

1. Select a disc from the DISC STAND.
2. Sit down at one of the phonographs in CARREL 1; put a headset on.
3. Plug headset cord into hole on top of phonograph, marked: headset.
4. Look at the label on your disc; if it reads:

   a) 33 1/3 RPM, turn the speed selector knob on the phonograph to 33 and the little lever on the tonearm (near needle) to LP.

   b) 45 RPM, turn the speed selector knob to 45 and the little lever on the tonearm to LP.

   c) 78 RPM, turn the speed selector knob to 78 and the little lever on the tonearm to 78.

5. Now write down the title of the disc. _____

6. Warm up the phonograph by turning the volume knob to *on.* (No! don't touch the tonearm yet!) The turntable will turn.
7. Don't skip what comes next:

   Sometimes you may want to listen only to a part of a disc. Many discs have different selections on them. They are on numbered bands listed on the label, like a table of contents in a book. If, for example, you want to hear only Band 3, put the tonearm down after the second shiny, ungrooved strip of the disc. Now follow instructions 8, 9, 10 and 11, and listen carefully.

8. Press the black button next to the tonearm rest. The turntable will stop.
9. *NOW:* Pick up the tonearm and gently place it where you want to begin.
10. Pull up the black button next to the tonearm rest and listen carefully.
11. When you have heard what you wanted to hear, press the black button next to the tonearm rest. Only lift the tonearm after the turntable has stopped moving. This way, the disc does not get scratched.

Lesson I, No. 3

12. Now answer the following questions as best you can:
   a) What kind of disc was this? (Check the word that describes it best.)
   ____Song, ____Music, ____Story, ____Poetry, ____Information, ____Dance.
   b) What interesting things did you hear? (Check one or more of the following.)
   ____New facts, ____New sounds, ____Rhythms, ____Instruments, anything else?

   _____

   Write it on this line, please.
   c) Would you recommend this disc to your teacher for use with your class some time this year?
   ____yes ____no
   d) If you checked YES, how do you think she could best use it? For:
   ____Entertainment, ____Enjoyment, ____Information about_____, _____
   if you have any other ideas, write

   _____

   them on this line please.
   e) If you checked NO, please explain why you think she could not use it.
   ____Too hard, ____Too childish, ____Not interesting,

   _____.

   other reason

Lesson I, No. 4   ELMWOOD MEDIA CENTER

8mm LOOP FILM REPORT   Name_____Class _____

To use an 8mm loop cartridge film for the first time, you need the help of the Media Specialist or Media Aide.

1. Ask the Media Specialist or Media Aide for the loop film you want. He will show you how they are organized for easy finding.
2. You will be shown individually how to insert the cartridge in the machine and how to operate it.
3. A loop film is without sound and continuous. See it a few times and then complete the following report.
   a) Title _____
   b) What is main topic of this loop film?

   _____

   c) Write very briefly what you found out when you viewed this film. Write each piece of information on a different line like this. Use as many lines as you need.

   _____
   _____
   _____
   _____
   _____

   d) Make a check mark in front of those lines you want to know more about. Ask help if you don't understand what to do.

ORGANIZATION OF MEDIA

Lesson II: Subject: THE DEWEY DECIMAL SYSTEM
OF MEDIA ORGANIZATION

Single class group meetings in the media center (schedule as many meetings as there are single class groups on this level)

Materials and Equipment: overhead projector, transparencies of Dewey Decimal System and Media Center Floor Map

Skills: Recall and use of media terminology
Reading Media Center Floor Map

Explanation of system of media organization by Dewey Decimal System, and color codings by Dewey Decimal classes on spines of books. With third- and fourth-year children, each child is given a large sign with a Dewey Class number or other designation to take to the place where the corresponding media are located. Including the signs for special areas like *Picture Books, Easy to Read Books, Fairy and Folk Tales* (398.2), *B* for Biography, *Recordings, Filmstrips, Film Loops, Periodicals, Reference Materials, Atlases, Dictionaries, Card Catalog, Faculty Shelves, Information File, Picture File, Study Print and Poster Case, Discs,* as many as 24 area signs can be devised. If your group is larger, make additional signs for *Charging Desk, Return Book Truck, Shelving Truck, A-V Room,* etc. If you don't have enough areas to identify, have the class team in groups of two.

MAP ACTIVITY

With sixth-year children, the media floor plan is projected on a map transparency. An explanation of how the class is to do the assignment on the map by matching the numbers to the appropriate areas is given. This is not as difficult as it seems because all areas are clearly marked with signs using the terminology listed on the map. (See illustration 5-1.) The maps are given to classroom teachers, who give them to each child, when convenient, during the following week, to do as an independent activity. Classroom follow-up: work with place value in decimals in arithmetic.

THE MEDIA CATALOG

Lesson III: Subject: THE CARD CATALOG; AS AN INDEX OF ALL MEDIA

Double class group meeting (schedule as many meetings as there are double classroom groups on this level)
Materials and Equipment: Filmstrip on use of conventional library card catalog; filmstrip machine; A-V catalog card transparency.
Skills: Note taking from filmstrip
Oral reporting from notes taken (ask children to take notes *only* on things they did not know before)

Present group with reasons for differences in media center card catalogs:

1. Why a divided catalog? (subject and author-title)

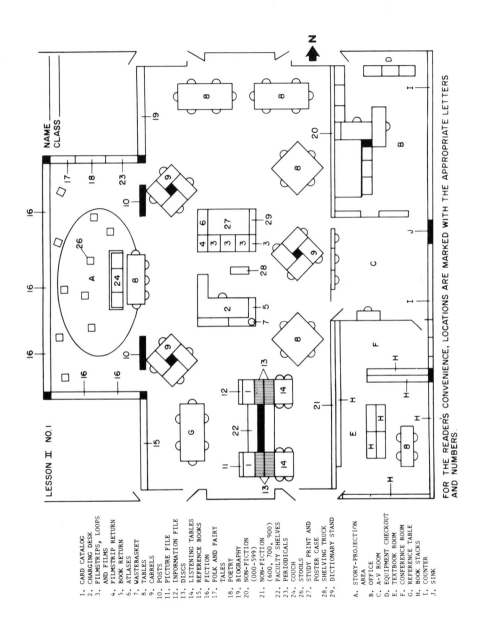

1. CARD CATALOG
2. CHARGING DESK
3. FILMSTRIPS, LOOPS
   AND FILMS
4. FILMSTRIP RETURN
5. BOOK RETURN
6. ATLASES
7. TABLES
8. WASTEBASKET
9. CARRELS
10. POSTS
11. PICTURE FILE
12. INFORMATION FILE
13. DISCS
14. LISTENING TABLES
15. REFERENCE BOOKS
16. FICTION
17. FOLK AND FAIRY
    TALES
18. POETRY
19. BIOGRAPHY
20. NON-FICTION
    (000-599)
21. NON-FICTION
    (600, 700, 900)
22. FACULTY SHELVES
23. PERIODICALS
24. COUCH
26. STOOLS
27. STUDY PRINT AND
    POSTER CASE
28. SHELVING TRUCK
29. DICTIONARY STAND

A. STORY-PROJECTION
   AREA
B. OFFICE
C. A-V ROOM
D. EQUIPMENT CHECKOUT
E. TEXTBOOK ROOM
F. CONFERENCE ROOM
G. REFERENCE TABLE
H. BOOK STACKS
I. COUNTER
J. SINK

FOR THE READER'S CONVENIENCE, LOCATIONS ARE MARKED WITH THE APPROPRIATE LETTERS AND NUMBERS.

Illustration 5-1.

2. Why color-coded cards for various media? Illustrate with transparency on one subject including different media on color-coded cards.

MEDIA CATALOG PUZZLES

Follow-ups:

The three puzzles which follow—FIND THE BIRDIE; SOME LIKE IT HOT, SOME LIKE IT COLD; and CATALOG—are fun activities which are designed to give lower and upper intermediate children practice in locating:

1. author cards in the author and title catalog
2. a book by subject and title
3. a specific title on an author card
4. a filmstrip by subject and title
5. locating titles directly, if the first word of the title is given.

Once the puzzles are completed, they may serve as reading lists. FIND THE BIRDIE can become a fiction reading list to go with a unit on birds. A second nonfiction list can be compiled in puzzle form, from your own media catalog to include recordings, filmstrips and film loops or whatever media are available in your media center. After completing the puzzles the finding of the materials gives practice in using the media card catalog and locating the media. Gathered by the children and organized for use in the classroom, they will be more intensively consulted than if the teacher or media specialist had collected them for the class.

For dessert: extra puzzles for avid puzzlers in which the same skills are served up with different icings are: ANIMAL TRAFFIC, also suitable for third- and fourth-year students; TOGETHERNESS; WHO IS WHO IN THIS ZOO?; NAME CALLING; and STRANGE CRITTERS. At the tail end: a child's best friend starring in: IT'S A DOG'S LIFE.

Lesson III, No. 1   ELMWOOD MEDIA CENTER

Intermediate

FIND THE BIRDIE

Birds are the subject of many stories. In the left column are titles with birds in them, but the birds have flown away. Find the missing bird(s), put them in their cages and match each title to its author, by putting the letter in front of the author's name before the title.

The first one is done for you as an example.

____K____   1. The Ugly [D|u|ck|l|in|g]   a. Taro Yashima

_____   2. [   ] in the Family   b. Maud Petersham

_____   3. Joel and the Wild [   ]   c. Keith Robertson

_____   4. Three Stuffed [   ]   d. Sarah O. Jewett

_____   5. White [   ]   e. T. Yamaguchi

_____   6. The Wild [   ]   f. Helga Sandburg

_____   7. The Golden [   ]   g. Richard Atwater

_____   8. [   ] Boy   h. Farley Mowat

_____   9. Mr. Popper's [   ]   i. Hugh Lofting

_____   10. Johnny [   ] 's Garden   j. Marjorie Flack

_____   11. The [   ] Crows   ✗. H. C. Andersen

_____   12. The Restless [   ]   l. Leslie Brooke

_____   13. Dr. Dolittle and the Green [   ]

P. S. One author has 2 books, that is why there are 13 titles and 12 authors.

Lesson III, No. 2   ELMWOOD MEDIA CENTER

Intermediate

SOME LIKE IT HOT, SOME LIKE IT COLD

Some books are hot, others cold. In the list of titles on the left, I have given you the hot or cold words. Each dash stands for another word of the title. The authors of these books are listed on the right, but not on the same line as the book they wrote.

Use the author and title catalog to figure out the titles and match the authors to their books as in the example on the first line.

(*c*) WINTER *Danger*   a. H. C. Anderson
(   ) _____SUMMER ___ ___ ___   b. Laura Ingalls Wilder
(   ) _____FIRE (one word)   X̶ William O. Steele
(   ) _____ _____ WINTER   d. Jerrold Beim
(   ) ____ _____ HOT ____ ____   e. Lynn Poole
(   ) BURNING _____   f. Phillip Viereck
(   ) ____ _____ ICE _____   g. Anico Surany
(   ) _____ ICEBERG _____   h. E. G. Valens
(   ) FLAMING _____   i. Jim Kjelgaard
(   ) _____ ICE   j. David O. Woodbury
(   ) ____ SUMMER SNOW _____   k. William O. Steele
(   ) _____ SNOW _____   l. Gene Zion
(   ) SNOW _____   m. Alan Delgado

Lesson III, No. 3

ELMWOOD MEDIA CENTER
Name: _____
Class: _____

Find one of each of these beginning with the letter in the box at left; one of the letters, A, is done as an example for you.

	A fiction book (title)	A science book (title)	A filmstrip on a subject that begins with:	An author's last name	A picture book (title)
C					
A	Adventures in Bangkok	All Around You	ANIMALS-HABITS AND BEHAVIOR: Mrs. Bear and her family	Aulaire	ABC Bunny
T					
A					
L					
O					
G					

Primary & Intermediate   ELMWOOD MEDIA CENTER

Name_____   Class_____

ANIMAL TRAFFIC

In each of the books whose titles are listed in the last column, an animal has, for an animal, a very unusual way of traveling. It will be your job to find out: *1. the animal's name* and *2. his means of transportation.* The titles are mixed up; you can use them as clues. If the title card does not have the information, find the book and look it up.

NAME	VEHICLE	TITLES
A mouse, _____, rides a_____.		The Story of Babar
A toad, _____, rides a_____.		The Story of Ping
A cat, _____, rides a_____.		The Mouse and the Motorcycle
A cricket, _____, rides a_____.		Space Cat
A monkey, _____, rides a_____.		The Wind in the Willows
A baby kangaroo whose mother's name is _____, rides a_____.		Stuart Little
A duck, _____, rides a_____.		Carbonel, the King of the Cats
A 2nd mouse, _____, rides a_____.		The Cricket in Times Square
Two elephants, on their honeymoon, 1. _____, 2. _____, ride a _____.		Anatole
Another cat, _____, rides a_____.		Curious George
A 3rd mouse, _____, rides a_____.		Katy No-Pocket

Intermediate   ELMWOOD MEDIA CENTER

                                          Name_____

                                          Class_____

TOGETHERNESS

Match the book characters below to their *authors* on the left and on the same line list the *title* in which they appear.

AUTHORS   CHARACTERS   TITLES

example: A. A. Milne_____Eeyore_____Winnie the Pooh

James Barrie_____

Laszlo Hamori_____

Jean de Brunhoff_____

Rudyard Kipling_____

Ian Fleming_____

Kate Seredy_____

Roald Dahl_____

Oliver Butterworth_____

Louisa May Alcott_____

Laura Ingalls Wilder_____

Michael Bond_____

Esther Forbes_____

Norton Juster_____

CHARACTERS: Paddington; Commander Crackpot; Milo; Amy March; Johnnie Tremain; Zephir; Jancsi; Almanzo; Charlie Bucket; Mowgli; Latsi; Nate Twitchell; Wendy Darling.

Intermediate   ELMWOOD MEDIA CENTER

Name_____ Class_____

WHO IS WHO
IN THIS ZOO?[1]

What kind of animal is each of these in the 1st column? In the 2nd column are your possible choices. Their authors are mixed up in the 3rd column. You can find all this by using the card catalog and by carefully reading the notes on the cards. Some you will know without looking them up. Look at the example on the first line and do it in the same way.

A. Mrs. Tiggy Winkle (10,h)	1. bull	a. Jean de Brunhoff
B. Aslan ( )	2. deer	b. Rudyard Kipling
C. Babar ( )	3. snake	c. Munro Leaf
D. Crictor ( )	4. donkey	d. C. S. Lewis
E. Bambi ( )	5. elephant	e. Hugh Lofting
F. Charlotte ( )	6. lion	f. A. A. Milne
G. Curious George ( )	7. mongoose	g. Sterling North
H. Eeyore ( )	8. parrot	h̶. Beatrix Potter
I. Polynesia ( )	9. raccoon	i. H. A. Rey
J. Rascal ( )	1̶0̶. hedgehog	j. Felix Salten
K. Rikki Tikki Tavi ( )	11. spider	k. E. B. White
L. Ferdinand ( )	12. monkey	l. Tomi Ungerer

[1]Adapted from "A Children's Bestiary," *Saturday Review,* March 15, 1969, p. 35. "Your Literary I.Q." David M. Glixon. Copyright 1969, Saturday Review, Inc.

Intermediate   ELMWOOD MEDIA CENTER

Name_____Class_____

NAME CALLING

The titles of the books below refer to the main character or characters in them. Can you find out what the names of these book characters are? Some of the characters have only first names, others first and last names. In titles with an underlined name, find the name of that person only.

Example:

The <u>Prince</u> and the Pauper   — Edward Tudor

The Little Princess   —
Weaver of Dreams   —
The Good Master   —
Fire Hunter   —
Plain Girl   —
The <u>youngest</u> of Little Women   —

Wilderness Bride   —
The Pigman   —
The Hobbit   —
Farmer Boy   —
The Little Lame Prince   —
My <u>Father's</u> Dragon   —

Intermediate   ELMWOOD MEDIA CENTER

Name_____ Class_____

STRANGE CRITTERS

Match the creatures in the left column with the author or character clues in the right. Some can be found by using the card catalog; for others try the *Reader's Encyclopedia,* the *Dictionary of Phrase and Fable* and if you have no luck with any of these, a poetry index like *Index to Children's Poetry* and its *Supplements.* This is not an easy puzzle. Take your time. When you are really stuck ask for help.

Critters	*Clues*
A. THE POBBLE	_____ H. C. Andersen
B. CHESHIRE CAT	_____ Dr. Seuss
C. ASLAN	_____ Finian's daughter
D. MR. TUMNUS, a faun	_____ Juno
E. OOBLECK	_____ Alice
F. PSAMMEAD	_____ Jonathan Swift
G. HOBBIT	_____ Dr. Dolittle
H. HOUYHNHNMS	_____ Reynard the Fox
I. PUSHMI-PULLYU	_____ C. S. Lewis
J. MERMAID	_____ Tolkien
K. CHANTICLEER	_____ Lewis Carroll
L. LEPRECHAUN	_____ Barnstable children
M. ARGUS	_____ Edward Lear
N. SNARK	_____ White witch

Intermediate   ELMWOOD MEDIA CENTER

Name_____ Class_____

IT'S A DOG'S LIFE

When people say: "It's a dog's life," they mean it's a hard life, but the dogs that belong to the owners on the left, in the books by the authors in the middle, don't feel that way for the most part. Who are these lucky dogs? Can you find their names and put them in the right column, on the same line as their owner and author?

Owners	*Authors*	*Dogs*
Dorothy	FRANK BAUM	_____
David	ELLEN TARRY	_____
Henry	BEVERLY CLEARY	_____
Duke	WILLIAM PENE DUBOIS	_____
John Thornton	JACK LONDON	_____
Fred	ROSEMARY WEIR	_____
Travis	FRED GIPSON	_____
Danny	JIM KJELGAARD	_____
Jase	ZACHARY BALL	_____
The Darlings	JAMES BARRIE	_____
Madeline	LUDWIG BEMELMANS	_____
Peter	EZRA JACK KEATS	_____
Miss Marvelous	MARGARET OTTO	_____

MEDIA CATALOG AS AN INFORMATION SOURCE

Lesson IV: Subject: THE MEDIA CARD CATALOG AS A SOURCE OF INFORMATION

Double class group meeting in classroom. (schedule as many meetings as there are double classroom groups on this level)

Materials and Equipment: Transparencies of author, title and subject cards of books; A-V materials, and pamphlet materials

Skills:

Observation

Deductive reasoning

Note taking from transparencies

Taking lecture notes

This lesson is planned as an observation contest. Children are divided in groups, for example, boys against girls, or class against class. The purpose is to list as many facts about a book as they can find on the transparency of a subject catalog card of that book, within a certain time limit. Children may team in groups of two, one child to take notes. Time is called by shutting off the overhead. On a blank transparency, the observations are listed, each group listing one in turn (by group). Each fact listed is worth one point. When as many facts as possible are listed (fiction, nonfiction, copyright date, publisher, subject, where found on the shelves, author, illustrator, number of pages, contents, bibliography, maps, music, picture book, easy to read, belongs to a series, has a sequel, is a sequel, edition, etc.) replace the transparency of the card on the overhead and have groups take turns pointing to the location of each listed fact on the card. Each group should verify its own findings on the card. For each improperly verified fact a point is lost. For repetition of a fact already mentioned, a penalty of two points is levied against the group who mentions it.

Finish by showing subject catalog cards of A-V media on the same subject. Show group how to make a bibliography of a book, a filmstrip and a pamphlet on one subject, on the overhead, from the transparencies used in this lesson.

Follow up: in small groups or by individuals:

Next day and every day for a week, children will make a working bibliography on their social studies topic, using the cross media bibliography sheet below.

CROSS MEDIA BIBLIOGRAPHY SHEET

Name_____

Social Studies Class_____

On your topic:

Find in the card catalog and list below:

1 non-fiction book of 120 pages or more, not more than 5 years old

1 fiction book, with illustrations, of 150 pages or more

1 pamphlet

1 filmstrip suitable for your age

1 record suitable for your age

List book here by:

Call #	Author (last name first)	Title	Publisher	copy-right date	No. of pgs.

List pamphlet here by:

Title	copy-right date

List filmstrip here by:

Call #	Title	Publisher	copy-right date (if given)

List record here by:

Call #	Title	Publisher

They will locate their materials to be placed on reserve for them in individual shoe boxes (labeled with their names) to be used during independent study.

6

Techniques and Activities for Implementing Media Instructional Goal Two: Children Learn to Use Media Material

PRIMARY RESEARCH AND REFERENCE

These techniques are introduced to second- and third-year students through the activity called LANDSMEN. The tool used is the encyclopedia. Finding facts about famous people is a good and simple way to introduce encyclopedias and to compare them. When the social studies curriculum in the second and third year deals with "the Local Community and County" and the "Greater Urban or Rural Area" it is easy to involve children in the cultural mix of their community by examining the cultural background of their own families and classmates.

Once they have done this, looking up a "landsman" in an encyclopedia and discovering his contribution to the area or country as a whole will be more meaningful.

Teacher and media specialist cull a list of "landsmen" from the curriculum and the media specialist pre-checks that they can be located in an encyclopedia. The simple question sheet which follows becomes the framework of the "research." Able children look the same person up in a number of encyclopedias and compare the information. So far the anthropological and sociological aspects of the unit are covered. To include the historical, a time line, decorated by the flags of the countries from which the "landsmen" came, makes for additional research, enjoyable art work and an understanding of time passing. Many other things can be done with the "landsmen" activity. Just one example: the contributions of the "landsmen" can be classified and put into groups such as the economic, cultural, and scientific. More media research can uncover comtemporary community leaders and look into their contributions.

LANDSMEN   ELMWOOD MEDIA CENTER

Name_____Class_____

My "Landsman" is_____

1. When was he/she born?_____

2. Can you figure out how old he/she was when he/she died?_____

3. Was he/she married?_____ If so, can you find his/her wife's/ husband's name? _____

4. Did he/she have any children? _____ How many?_____

5. Why did he/she become famous?_____
_____

6. Write down one *other* interesting fact about him/her._____
_____
_____

7. Write the title, volume no. (V. no.), and page no. (p.) of the encyclopedia in which you found your information.

_____,_____,_____
    title   V. no.   p.

REFERENCE CONTESTS AND ACTIVITIES

For older children a reference contest between class groups aimed at the utilization of indexes in encyclopedias, the following up of "see" and "see also" references and the comparing of all available encyclopedia sets in the media center, is another painless way to involve teachers and children. The teaching of documentation of sources is built into the game by faulting all undocumented answers. Only encyclopedias may be used. The name of the game is INDEX HUNT (see below), because the majority of the answers can only be located by using the index. In many instances, the answers can be found in the index only, specifically in the *Compton's* and *Britannica Junior's* fact-finding type of index. Children who pick up the *Worldbook* soon find out that following up the cross references is a must.

Each question has a point value, indicated by a number in the left-hand corner. The questions are dittoed off and cut into strips, one question on each strip. Each of the teachers involved puts a boxful of strips on his desk. The children do the questions in the media center as an independent activity, one question at a time. The answered questions labeled with name and class are dropped in a box at the charging desk in the media center. The time limit is three weeks. As soon as a class has used up a box of questions, a new batch is provided. No child may answer the same question more than once. Questions without names are voided. The media specialist keeps the score and the class with the highest number of points wins. The prize is a party with a special interest film and of course refreshments.

INDEX HUNT[1]   ELMWOOD MEDIA CENTER

---

3   Q. What animal can break off its tail and grow a new one?
     A. _____
     Source: T. _____ V. _____ c. _____ p. _____

---

5   Q. Why were our great-great-great-grandmothers afraid to eat
        tomatoes?
     A. _____
     Source: T. _____ V. _____ c. _____ p. _____

---

3   Q. Does handling toads cause warts?
     A. _____
     Source: T. _____ V. _____ c. _____ p. _____

---

2   Q. How long does a box turtle live?
     A. _____
     Source: T. _____ V. _____ c. _____ p. _____

---

2   Q. Are vitamins food?
     A. _____
     Source: T. _____ V. _____ c. _____ p. _____

---

1. INDEX HUNT questions were selected from *Compton's Pictured Encyclopedia,* 1970. "Interest Questions Answered In This Volume" Vols. 1-15.

__4__ Q. Where is the world's largest reflecting telescope?

A. _____

Source: T. _____ V. _____ c. _____ p. _____

__1__ Q. Which continent is the home of the tiger?

A. _____

Source: T. _____ V. _____ c. _____ p. _____

__4__ Q. How do ants defend themselves?

A. _____

Source: T. _____ V. _____ c. _____ p. _____

__3__ Q. Which bird has the greatest wingspread?

A. _____

Source: T. _____ V. _____ c. _____ p. _____

__3__ Q. In which states is Arbor Day celebrated in winter?

A. _____

Source: T. _____ V. _____ c. _____ p. _____

__5__ Q. At what time of day did the ancient Greeks give theatrical performances?

A. _____

Source: T. _____ V. _____ c. _____ p. _____

__5__ Q. What president of the United States later became Chief Justice of the Supreme Court?

A. _____

Source: T. _____ V. _____ c. _____ p. _____

__4__ Q. Why do today's soldiers wear dull-colored uniforms?

A. _____

Source: T. _____ V. _____ c. _____ p. _____

__5__ Q. Why do leaves change color in the fall?

A. _____

Source: T. _____ V. _____ c. _____ p. _____

__4__ Q. Of which bridge in the U.S. is the main span 1212 feet long?

A. _____

Source: T. _____ V. _____ c. _____ p. _____

<u>3</u>   Q. What is the name of the largest lake in the world?

A. _____

Source: T. _____V. _____ c. _____ p. _____

<u>4</u>   Q. Which is the longest passenger railroad tunnel in the world?

A. _____

Source: T. _____V. _____ c. _____ p. _____

<u>5</u>   Q. Who was Vice-President when Lincoln was President?

A. _____

Source: T. _____V. _____ c. _____ p. _____

<u>3</u>   Q. When did the Saint Louis Cardinals last win the World Series?

A. _____

Source: T. _____V. _____ c. _____ p. _____

<u>4</u>   Q. What insects keep slaves?

A. _____

Source: T. _____ V. _____ c. _____ p. _____

<u>3</u>   Q. What do parasol ants grow for food?

A. _____

Source: T. _____ V. _____ c. _____ p. _____

<u>2</u>   Q. Which is colder, the Arctic or the Antarctic?

A. _____

Source: T. _____V. _____ c. _____ p. _____

<u>1</u>   Q. What is the "Christ of the Andes"?

A. _____

Source: T. _____ V. _____ c. _____ p. _____

<u>5</u>   Q. What was the Gordian knot?

A. _____

Source: T. _____V. _____ c. _____ p. _____

<u>2</u>   Q. According to legend, how did King Arthur prove his right to the throne?

A. _____

Source: T. _____ V. _____ c. _____ p. _____

<u>4</u>   Q. Why were spiders (Arachnidae) named for a mythical girl?

A. _____

Source: T. _____ V. _____ c. _____ p. _____

<u>1</u>   Q. Where does the bottle tree grow and why is it so called?

A. _____

Source: T. _____ V. _____ c. _____ p. _____

<u>3</u>   Q. How does Los Angeles get its water supply?

A. _____

Source: T. _____ V. _____ c. _____ p. _____

<u>3</u>   Q. Why is the Pacific Ocean bluer than the Atlantic?

A. _____

Source: T. _____ V. _____ c. _____ p. _____

<u>2</u>   Q. How did Mark Twain get his name?

A. _____

Source: T. _____ V. _____ c. _____ p. _____

<u>1</u>   Q. How can you tell Poison Ivy from Virginia Creeper?

A. _____

Source: T. _____ V. _____ c. _____ p. _____

<u>5</u>   Q. How much water may a medium-sized apple tree soak up on one summer day?

A. _____

Source: T. _____ V. _____ c. _____ p. _____

<u>5</u>   Q. What are the four differences between a plant and an animal?

A. _____

Source: T. _____ V. _____ c. _____ p. _____

<u>2</u>   Q. How long is a newly hatched alligator?

A. _____

Source: T. _____ V. _____ c. _____ p. _____

<u>5</u>   Q. Of what wood are baseball bats made?

A. _____

Source: T. _____ V. _____ c. _____ p. _____

1   Q. What is a sampler?
      A. _____
      Source: T. _____ V. _____ c. _____ p. _____

4   Q. When and where was Arbor Day first celebrated?
      A. _____
      Source: T. _____ V. _____ c. _____ p. _____

2   Q. What is a trundle bed? Find a picture.
      A. _____
      Source: T. _____ V. _____ c. _____ p. _____

4   Q. What animals live from 30-40 years?
      A. _____
      Source: T. _____ V. _____ c. _____ p. _____

2   Q. What kind of food does an armadillo eat?
      A. _____
      Source: T. _____ V. _____ c. _____ p. _____

3   Q. What is another name for a carrier pigeon?
      A. _____
      Source: T. _____ V. _____ c. _____ p. _____

1   Q. Where did the tomato come from?
      A. _____
      Source: T. _____ V. _____ c. _____ p. _____

4   Q. Who discovered the X-ray?
      A. _____
      Source: T. _____ V. _____ c. _____ p. _____

5   Q. Find the name of a plant that eats insects.
      A. _____
      Source: T. _____ V. _____ c. _____ p. _____

4   Q. If you like chocolate you should be grateful to the _____
         _____who first used it as a drink.
      Source: T. _____ V. _____ c. _____ p. _____

A number of teachers have picked up this specific question method and tailored it to subject matter. They have used it to launch a unit, practice note taking and for open-book tests. HISTORIC OPPONENTS (see below) is a history hunt with encyclopedia, biographical dictionary, or Benet's *Reader's Encyclopedia.*

Intermediate   ELMWOOD MEDIA CENTER

Name_____ Class_____

HISTORIC OPPONENTS

All of these characters fought against each other; some in battles, others with words. Who opposed whom? Match opponents by putting the numbers in the correct parentheses

(The first one is done as an example.)

Hannibal	(*18*)	1. Brutus
Lee	( )	2. Houston
Custer	( )	3. Achilles
Santa Ana	( )	4. Montagues
Douglas	( )	5. Disraeli
Cornwallis	( )	6. Wellington
Burgoyne	( )	7. Aaron Burr
Caesar	( )	8. Montezuma
Cortez	( )	9. Philip of Macedon
Pershing	( )	10. Antiochus Epiphanes
Napoleon	( )	11. Washington
Monitor	( )	12. Kennedy
Hector	( )	13. Sitting Bull
Cyrus the Great	( )	14. Gates
Saladin	( )	15. Hindenburg
Gladstone	( )	16. Lincoln
Nixon	( )	17. Merrimac
Pizarro	( )	X. Scipio
Judas Maccabeus	( )	19. Richard the Lion-Hearted
Demosthenes	( )	20. Atahualpa
Capulets	( )	21. Grant
Alexander Hamilton	( )	22. Croesus

NAME THEIR FAME (see below) is a contest with three levels of sophistication. Second-year children who have completed the LANDS-MEN can compete without frustration by using encyclopedias. Older children need to refer to biographical dictionaries and other special tools.

On a bulletin board, labeled pictures of 15 men and women are displayed. They are from many different cultures and fields of endeavor. On the simplest level the children only locate five of these in encyclopedias, but as not everyone can be found there, they have to proceed by trial and error until they find five that are listed. Of course they may try the other reference books on display under the bulletin board. (None of these may be taken from the room for the duration of the contest.)

The next level is for third- and fourth-year intermediate children who choose 8 from the 15 to investigate. They must document their sources and use a biographical subject card in the card catalog to find a filmstrip, record or book about one of the subjects.

Fifth- and sixth-year children have to cover the whole list, document their sources, use a biographical subject card in the card catalog and take brief notes on one of the featured men and women. The contest is open to anyone who is interested.

NAME THEIR FAME informally introduces *The Concise Dictionary of American Biography, Current Biography Yearbook* (1963-), *Webster's Biographical Dictionary, Junior Authors* and *More Junior Authors, Negro Makers of History* and *The Negro Almanac*, in which all fifteen subjects can be found. Of course the card catalog may be used as well. Each successful contestant earns a piece of chocolate cake iced with the names of "the 15." Count the winners, then bake enough cake to fête all! Now give everyone A SPORTING CHANCE (page 135) to use all reference tools introduced so far.

NAME THEIR FAME   Elmwood Media Center
Contest No. 1
                              Name_____ Class_____

Win a piece of BIOGRAPHY CAKE!

Rules: A. Find out why five of the people whose pictures are on
           display are famous
        B. Write or print clearly

1. _____is famous because_____
   (person's name)
   _____

2. _____is famous because_____
   (person's name)
   _____

3. _____is famous because_____
   (person's name)
   _____

4. _____is famous because_____
   (person's name)
   _____

5. _____is famous because_____
   (person's name)
   _____

NAME THEIR FAME   Elmwood Media Center
Contest No. 2

Name_____Class_____

Win a piece of BIOGRAPHY CAKE!

Rules: A.   Find out the fame of eight of the people whose pictures are on display.

      B.   Document your answer (this means that you must list your *source* and *page number.*)

      C.   Use the card catalog to find one book, filmstrip or record, about one of these men or women. List it by its author and title at the end.

1. _____, _____
     (person's name)   (fame)

     (source)

2. _____, _____
     (person's name)   (fame)

     (source)

3. _____, _____
     (person's name)   (fame)

     (source)

4. _____, _____
     (person's name)   (fame)

     (source)

5. _____, _____
     (person's name)   (fame)

     (source)

6. _____, _____
     (person's name)   (fame)

     (source)

7. _____, _____
     (person's name)   (fame)

     (source)

8. _____, _____
     (person's name)   (fame)

     (source)

Book, filmstrip or record found: _____

NAME THEIR FAME   Elmwood Media Center

Contest No. 3   Name_____ Class_____

Win a piece of BIOGRAPHY CAKE!

Rules: A. Research the fame of all 15 persons whose pictures are on display.
         B. Find year of birth for all and year of death for those no longer living.
         C. Use the card catalog to find a book, filmstrip or record by or about one of the men and one of the women. List both at end by author and title.
         D. Choose the person who interested you the most and in one paragraph describe his character (what kind of person he was). Use other side of paper.

Name of person	Fame	Life span	Source
Addams, Jane			
Anderson, Marian			
Audubon, John J.			
Bunche, Ralph			
Drew, Charles			
Evers, Medgar			
Gershwin, George			
Harris, Patricia			
Hughes, Langston			
Marshall, Thurgood			
Matisse, Henri			
Mayo (Brothers)			
Price, Leontyne			
Thurber, James			
Wilkins, Roy			

Book, filmstrip or record found:_____

Book, filmstrip or record found:_____

Intermediate   ELMWOOD MEDIA CENTER

Name_____Class_____

A SPORTING CHANCE

You'll have a sporting chance to find out what each of this "baker's dozen" of sportsmen and -women was famous for, if you use the right reference tool. Also try a new one: *The Encyclopedia of Sports.* You may know one or two without looking them up; if you're not sure, check! Put the number in front of each person next to his (her) sport please.

1. Althea Gibson	wrestling
2. Gertrude Ederle	swimming
3. Sonia Henie	boxing
4. Johnnie Weismueller	football
5. Annie Oakley	baseball
6. Babe Didrikson Zaharias	tennis—men's singles
7. Zabriskie Brothers	figure skating
8. Jack Johnson	golf
9. Jessie Owens	channel swimming
10. Jim Brown	tennis—women's singles
11. Norkay Tensing	track
12. Arthur Ashe	sharpshooting
13. Hank Greenberg	mountaineering

QUIZ CONTESTS

IDENTIFICATION and MINI-QUIZZES are always in evidence in the media center. Only a small amount of space is required for either; it is a good idea always to post them in the same place so that the children become accustomed to look there. Two weeks duration for these is ideal, alternating them weekly.

MINI-QUIZZES (pages 137-139) are good for primary children, because they consist of a single question. Many of them are designed to familiarize the children with various aspects of the media center collection. When necessary, clues are provided. It is general policy not to give professional help with any of the contests; however, children may help each other and when they find the answer together, each one submits the answer on his own slip. Here follow a few examples of some that require educated guesses and others which need to be looked up:

How many books do we have in the media center? (the closest guess wins; remember to include books that are out!)

For A-J classes only!

How many encyclopedia sets of ten volumes or more do we have in the media center?

Find the exact number of records we have on HOLIDAYS. For more MINI-QUIZZES see the following MINI-QUIZ list.

IDENTIFICATION QUIZZES are really quick reference quizzes. There are many possibilities. Begin in the fall of the year with a flower, leaf and seed or fruit identification game. Call it TEST YOUR FLOWER POWER (page 140). Collected seed pods, fall foliage and wild flowers are displayed in a vase and on a bulletin board behind it. Give each stem a numbered label and ditto off entry forms with numbered lines, and a source line. Next to the vase display the nature study guides and tree and flower identification books in which the answers can be found. To be considered a winner documentation must be complete. The prize is an appearance on the school intercom, live or on tape, with a short program describing, e.g. the characteristics of the identified plants, and including some pertinent nature poetry, original or looked up.

PLAY THE SHELL GAME, FIND THE RIGHT NAME (page 141) is another good contest to schedule after the summer vacation. In a small space on a shallow baking sheet, sprinkle beach sand and perhaps drape a fishing net, if available. On the sand place about

20-30 shells. Clearly number each one with a fine-point, indelible magic marker. Expect that some of the most attractive ones will disappear, in spite of this. Keep on collecting new ones. Many children will offer duplicates from their collections. Shells may also be picked up quite inexpensively. Collections of foreign coins picked up while traveling, stamps, wildlife conservation stickers which often come in the mail, an insect collection all lend themselves to a contest of this kind.

A collection of travel posters usually yields some with photographs of famous buildings or other landmarks, such as Stonehenge or the Blarney Stone. A poster of the Acropolis with just the word Greece as clue, or Big Ben with only the slogan "Visit London" are good for contests on two levels. Primary children only need to identify the building in question; intermediate children are asked to contribute a thumbnail sketch giving some information about it in their own words. Calendars of airlines usually are good sources for this type of architectural quiz, which would be a joint effort of the art teacher and the media specialist. Art identification contests are equally successful and stimulate an interest in art and an acquaintance with artists. A collection of art reproductions of interest to children is needed as a resource plus the art reference books to identify them.

ELMWOOD MEDIA CENTER

MINI QUIZZES—I

For each quiz question the answer is written on a slip and dropped into a box.

How many books do you think get lost during a year in our Media Center?

From what periodicals can you learn about other countries? List all the titles.

How many poetry records do we have?

What is folklore?

What is mythology?

Find the Dewey Decimal number for Dinosaurs.*

How many books do you think we have in our Media Center? (Don't forget the ones that are out!) The closest guess wins.

*Ages 6-8 only

How many encyclopedia sets of 10 volumes or more do we have in the Media Center?*

How many filmstrips on insects do we have?

Find one biography on a sound filmstrip and write it down. (the title)

What is the name of the machine that projects a picture from a book? Opaque projector or overhead projector?*

List three biographies of sportsmen and/or -women.

Find three poems on Thanksgiving.

Who said: "Work consists of whatever a body is obliged to do. Play consists of whatever a body is not obliged to do."

Who said: "If I can stop one heart from breaking, I shall not live in vain."

Who said: "They gave it me for an un-birthday present."

Who said: "When the frost is on the pumpkin."

Who said: "There is no frigate like a book to take us lands away."

When you wish to use a very large book, which is the best way?*
    use two hands to carry it to a table
    ask a friend to help you carry it
    slide it off the shelf and use it on the floor
    make a space on the shelf and open it there

The Newbery Medal Books are owned by most libraries because—*
    they are named for a famous author who liked children
    each won the award as a distinguished book
    they are written by famous historians
    libraries get them free

MINI QUIZZES—II

A bibliography is—
    a collection of articles
    a list of books
    the life story of a person
    a list of words

Which of the things listed is *not* on the title page of a book?*
    publisher
    author
    illustrator

*Ages 6-8 only

title

copyright date

Which one of the following things is never indicated in a book?*
the date of the information in the book
what the book is about
why the book was written
how long it will take to read the book

The call number has been called the "key" to the library. In which places below will you be sure to find this key written?
on the 50th page of each book in the library
on the card in the card catalog
on each shelf of the library
on the spine of each book

A Dewey Decimal classification number is the symbol for—
the subject
the title
the price
the author
the grade

If a catalog card has the top line printed in capital letters, that means the book is—
about that subject
by that person
known by that title
published by that company

The articles in *World Book Encyclopedia* and *Compton's Pictured Encyclopedia* are arranged—*
in the order in which things happened
alphabetically by subject
in the order of importance of subjects
with related topics placed together
none of these

Cross references in an encyclopedia refer you to—
useful reference books
other articles on topics related to the one you are reading
other encyclopedias
other articles on the same topic
all of the above

*Ages 6-8 only

ELMWOOD MEDIA CENTER

Name_____ Class_____

TEST YOUR FLOWER POWER

1. Answer: _____
   Source: _____
       last name of   title   page
       author

2. Answer:_____
   Source:_____
       a.   t.   p.

3. Answer:_____
   Source:_____
       a.   t.   p.

4. Answer:_____
   Source:_____
       a.   t.   p.

5. Answer:_____
   Source:_____
       a.   t.   p.

6. Answer:_____
   Source:_____
       a.   t.   p.

7. Answer:_____
   Source:_____
       a.   t.   p.

ELMWOOD MEDIA CENTER

Name_____ Class_____

PLAY THE SHELL GAME, FIND THE RIGHT NAME

Name of shell: *Source:*

1._____

               author (last name)   title   page

2. _____
3. _____
4. _____
5. _____
6. _____
7. _____
8. _____
9. _____
10. _____
11. _____
12. _____
13. _____
14. _____
15. _____
16. _____
17. _____
18. _____
19. _____
20. _____

HOLIDAY QUIZZES

At holiday times, topical games are very popular. A research quiz on why Lincoln grew a beard after he was elected president celebrates his birthday. With the book copier a "before" and "after" picture of Lincoln is made. Again, as always, the answer must be documented. The prize is a slice of home-made Lincoln Log. George Washington's birthday is a good time to expose the myth of the cherry tree with the question: Who made up the story of George Washington and the cherry tree? The prize? A piece of cherry pie, of course! Brotherhood week is good timing for the previously mentioned NAME THEIR FAME CONTEST.

For Halloween, MONSTER GALLERY and A MESSAGE FROM THE MEDIUM introduce the contestants to Benet's *Reader's Encyclopedia, Roget's Thesaurus, Webster's Dictionary of Synonyms* and *Brewer's Dictionary of Phrase and Fable.* Bookweek leads to books via the card catalog and the puzzles: WHERE ARE THE TITLES (primary) and FIND YOUR HIDDEN BOOKWEEK READING LIST (intermediate). The primary puzzle: THE MAGIC NUMBER THREE is for those primary children who have not yet had experience with the card catalog (page 147-151).

More reference work with dictionary and encyclopedia is hidden in two WINTER HOLIDAY QUIZZES (pages 152-153), again one on the primary and the other on the intermediate level. Because it is practically impossible to put Christmas, Hanukkah and New Year books on reserve at this time of the year, the quizzes are geared to the dictionary and encyclopedia.

When Lincoln was running for president, some- one suggested that if he grew a beard, he would get more votes.

He grew a beard **after** he was elected. Can you find the name of the person who gave him the idea?

2. Lincoln "Before"—from McNeer, May, *America's Abraham Lincoln,* illustrations by Lynd Ward; Houghton Mifflin Co., 1957, p. 69.

3. Lincoln "After"—from Ostendorff, Lloyd, *A Picture of Abraham Lincoln;* Lothrop, 1966, (frontispiece).

Who made up the story about George Washington and the Cherry Tree?

4. Reproduced from *George Washington* by Ingri and Parin d'Aulaire. Copyright 1936 by Doubleday and Company, Inc. Reprinted by permission of Doubleday and Company, Inc.

HALLOWEEN   ELMWOOD MEDIA CENTER

Name ————————————————Class————

A MESSAGE FROM THE MEDIUM TO THE MASSEURS

Dear teachers:

I am planning a Halloween display window titled:

"What scary creatures might you meet,
When you go for trick or treat?"

The display area will be covered with black paper from which all kinds of eyes will follow you wherever you go.

I would like to solicit names of all kinds of scary creatures from the children, and have them write the names in the display. These names can be found by looking up synonyms for all the names they can think of or find in literature selections, in dictionaries, the thesaurus and the synonym dictionaries. I have already found more than 150 such synonyms.

The child who contributes the most names of scary creatures will get a Halloween treat at our Halloween party. Each child who contributes a different (that is, not previously contributed) name may write it in the display. He should drop the name on a piece of paper, signed by himself, in the round "name-drop" envelope on the Halloween Quiz in the Media Center. Scary literary characters such as Dracula, Merlin and others are most welcome, too.

In this way, I hope to make the children aware of the large vocabulary of the supernatural which exists in literature. Maybe you can incorporate this activity in your language arts program this witching month?

Spookily,
Your Medium

Miriam

HALLOWEEN   ELMWOOD MEDIA CENTER

Name_____ Class_____

MONSTER GALLERY

In the left-hand column are monsters and creatures you would rather not meet on a dark night. If you were in the company of one of the characters in the right column, you might feel safer. To find out why, match them to the characters who conquered them or neutralized their powers.

Monsters	\ *Their Masters*
( ) The Cyclops, Polyphemus	a. David
( ) Minotaur	b. Arthur
( ) Cerberus	c. Oedipus
( ) Goliath	d. Sinbad
( ) Geryon	e. Beowulf
( ) Medusa	f. Theseus
( ) Merlin	g. Hercules
( ) Fafner	h. Perseus
( ) Grendel	i. Ulysses
( ) Roc	j. Orpheus
( ) Sphinx	k. Siegfried

BOOKWEEK   ELMWOOD MEDIA CENTER

Primary   Name_____Class_____

THE MAGIC NUMBER 3

In stories and poems many things come in threes. From the clues can you find out who these threesomes were?

Names of Peter Rabbit's 3 sisters and brothers:

_____

These 3 lost something and could not have any pie:

_____

Names of 3 boys who have adventures together in books by Nan H. Agle:

_____

3 animals in a silly poem by Edward Lear; one had a ring in his nose:

_____

3 Mother Goose characters who went sailing in a tub:

_____

A girl with golden hair wandered into their house:

_____

Each of these 3 animals tried to build a house but only one succeeded:

_____

These 3 animals together get rid of their enemy who lives under a bridge:

_____

3 whose tails were going to be cut off:

_____

BOOKWEEK   ELMWOOD MEDIA CENTER

primary   Name _____ Class _____

WHERE ARE THE TITLES?

There are 45 book titles hidden in this story puzzle. All of them are titles of books we have in our media center. You will know some of them; the others you can find by looking them up in the author and title cabinet of the card catalog. *Underline* each title neatly wherever you find it in the story. Some titles are mentioned twice. After BOOKWEEK the answers and the winners will be posted.

"If I ran the zoo, it would be a funny thing," said Madeline to Oliver, Frances and Julius, as they picked blueberries for Sal, over in the meadow, one morning in Maine. "Sure would," answered Lentil her big brother. Madeline did not pay any attention to him. She went on: "I would have friendly animals, like Babar the little elephant and millions and millions of cats and Angus and the ducks in my zoo." Julius piped up with: "What about some wild animals?"

"Oh sure," said Madeline; I will have millions and millions of bears and best of all, the biggest bear in the world! I'll ask a tiger called Thomas and Ferdinand the bull." "Aren't you going to have any monkeys in your zoo?" asked Oliver. "Of course I am; I'll have so many that curious George will say: 'Put me in the zoo please,' and I'll put him in charge of all the monkeys. I'll invite the elephant who liked to smash small cars and sleeps under a flying patchwork quilt. Animals from everywhere will come to a birthday party in my zoo, on Frances' birthday. We'll have a regular animal frolic, all day long. Pancakes for breakfast, hundreds and hundreds of pancakes! We better watch the biggest bear, so he won't drink up all the maple syrup; you know how he loves it! We'll eat outside so Ferdinand can smell the flowers. Three little pigs, the three billy goats Gruff, Peter Rabbit and Harry the dirty dog will square dance. Timothy Turtle will dance a jig. When the rooster crows, an ape in a cape will do a tumbling act. Then my father's dragon will serve stone soup and all the animals will get a sugarplum. And do you know what I'll do? I'll ask you to come and have fun." "Thank you," said Oliver, "but we better hurry, hurry, down, down the mountain; it is bedtime for Frances!"

BOOKWEEK ELMWOOD MEDIA CENTER

Intermediate Name _____Class_____

FIND YOUR HIDDEN BOOKWEEK READING LIST! *

In the story below 41 fiction book titles are hidden. Use the author and title section of the card catalog to find them. Underline *each exact title*. If you like, make two copies, one to hand in, the other to use as a reading list. Contest closes last day before Thanksgiving recess. Winners will be posted by Dec. 1.

— —

I, Juan de Pareja, was sitting on the swing in the summer house on my side of the mountain thinking about Alvin's secret code.

It was dark and I sensed there would be a storm from the west. What was that sound? Was it the nightbirds on Nantucket? The lightning looked like flaming arrows. Suddenly, I saw the shadow of a bull. The winter danger was real and I knew that ready or not I must take the trail through danger to the Hobbit.

My first thought was to take Harriet the spy, a true daughter of the mountains, with me. It was going to be a dangerous journey and we would need supplies from Henry Reed, Inc. A dog on Barkham Street growled fiercely and the Seventeenth Street Gang was after us. Thank goodness for Charlie and the chocolate factory. He had left the door open by mistake and we were able to avoid the whirling shapes that were being hurled at us.

After a while we were able to set out again. There were no boats on Bannermere, as a result of the big wave, so we were forced to go by secret railway.

We left the train at the family grandstand. There was silence over Dunkerque as we moved along the trail. What was that shining in the dark? It was Lotte's locket. Ahead of us was the empty schoolhouse. As we quietly advanced, we saw a family of foxes disappear into their lair.

The trail became steeper and we didn't feel like captains courageous anymore. Suddenly, Harriet screamed "landside!" and she disappeared from sight. This adventure was certainly more exciting than all those put together in the summer I was lost. As I went on doggedly, I stumbled upon five boys in a cave, the undergrounders,

*With thanks to volunteer parent Marion Schwartz who wrote the puzzle story.

and asked about Miguel. They said he had disappeared the night of the wall. It was too much. First Harriet, . . . and now Miguel.

I was the survivor, the loner. I knew I had to continue on my way. The moon shone like a banner in the sky. The owl was the winged watchman. I was on my way to an adventure in Bangkok.

What a wonderful, terrible time!

A WINTER HOLIDAY QUIZ   ELMWOOD MEDIA CENTER

(primary)   Name _____ Class _____

1. Name a state in the U.S. where poinsettias grow wild.

   _____

2. What is a syllabub? _____

   _____

3. What is a dreidel? _____

   _____

4. Does plum pudding have plums in it? _____
5. How many candles does a menorah have?_____
6. What is a posada?_____

   _____

7. Find another name for Santa Claus. K____ K _____
8. What is the name of the French Santa Claus? _____

   _____

9. In Sweden gifts are brought by the Y__T_____
10. In different countries children leave different foods for Santa Claus. In the U.S. he finds _____
    In Holland his horse finds _____
11. In Mexico Christmas goodies and small presents are hidden in a

    _____

12. Where did the Maccabees live? _____
13. What is a manger? _____

    _____

14. Does mincemeat have meat in it? _____

A WINTER HOLIDAY QUIZ   ELMWOOD MEDIA CENTER
(intermediate)
                    Name_____ Class_____

1. What is the scientific name of the Christmas rose?_____
   _____

2. Why does not every holly tree have red berries?_____
   _____

3. How long was the Yule Log supposed to burn?_____
4. What do the Hebrew letters on the Dreidel stand for?_____
   _____

5. The sale of Christmas seals is for the benefit of_____
   _____

6. What special food is eaten at Hanukkah time?_____
   _____

7. Where did the feeding of the birds on Christmas day originate?
   _____

8. In our country Christmas gifts are brought by Santa Claus,
   in Mexico by the_____
   in Japan by_____
   in China by_____
   in Denmark by_____
   in Holland by_____
   in Germany by_____
9. What is the name of the family which led the fight for freedom
   of the Jews against the Syrians?_____
10. Why is the month of January named after the Roman god
    Janus?_____
11. Why do we make noise on New Year's Eve?_____
    _____

12. What was the "miracle" of Hanukkah?_____
    _____
    _____

13. What is wassailing?_____

14. The name of the Syrian king against whom the Jews rebelled was
    _____

DICTIONARY GAMES

The usual ongoing dictionary work in the classroom covers the finding of synonyms, the meaning of words in the correct context, proper spelling of words and origins of words and phrases. BEASTLY SYNONYMS is beastly but not in the usual sense. Some of the words here must be "ferreted out" by "dogging" the trail from one meaning to another. Any unabridged dictionary, *The American Heritage Dictionary, Webster's Dictionary of Synonyms,* or *Roget's Thesaurus* will yield the answers. BEASTLY SYNONYMS (page 155) is an activity sheet for children who enjoy words and don't give up readily.

IN VOWEL LANGUAGE (page 156) it is strictly clean digging for words which contain all the possible vowel combinations in the English language. WORD OF THE MONTH (page 157) is based on the abbreviations of the 12 months which are hidden in the words to be looked up. PUT IN YOUR MONEY'S WORTH (page 158) contains hidden treasure; and last but not least is FOR THE BIRDS (page 159), early and late who will find it not so easy to catch the worm.

Exploration of figurative language, word and phrase origins, proverbs and allusions is another rewarding language arts activity. It is fun to explore *People Words* by Bill Severn, *Words from the Myths* by Isaac Asimov, *The Abecedarian Book,* by C.W. Ferguson, Samuel Epstein's *First Book of Words* and *Horsefeathers and Other Curious Words* by C. E. Funk. WHAT DO WE MEAN AND WHERE DID WE BORROW? (page 160) has been gathered from *Brewer's Dictionary of Phrase and Fable;* similarly the books mentioned above should yield many words to use in challenging dictionary games. THREE IS NOT A CROWD HERE (page 161) is a game for allusion dictionaries, such as *Brewer's* and Benet's. Many allusive phrases may be drawn from current reading and construed as a reference game before the selection is read in class. For pure fun try WHEN YOU THINK OF ONE, YOU THINK OF THE OTHER (page 162).

Intermediate   ELMWOOD MEDIA CENTER

Name_____ Class_____

BEASTLY SYNONYMS[5]

The idea of this word game is to fill the blanks with names of animals whose names have the same meaning and spelling as the verb defined alongside. (example: squeal or betray—rat)

to imitate —_____

to dismay — _____

to carry — _____

to harass — _____

to scold — _____

to devour — _____

to joke — _____

to find fault — _____

to guide — _____

to eat greedily —_____

to close tightly — _____

to trail persistently — _____

to take more than one's share — _____

to fool around — _____

to press or force into place — _____

to grouch —_____

---

[5]"Beastly Synonyms," adapted from "Beastly Verbs." *Saturday Review,* June 14, 1969, p. 35. "Your Literary I.Q." David M. Glixon. Copyright 1969, Saturday Review, Inc.

ELMWOOD MEDIA CENTER

Intermediate   Name_____ Class_____

VOWEL LANGUAGE[6]

The 25 vowel combinations below represent every possible arrangement of 2 vowels in the English language. Find the words in which they occur by looking up the definitions for each word on the right. Each dash stands for one letter.

1. _ _ aa _   —South African name for enclosed village or corral
2. ae _ _ _ _   —antenna
3. _ ai _   —bucket
4. _ _ ao _   —disorder
5. _ au _ _ _   —clumsy
6. _ ea _   —guide
7. _ ee _   —type of onion
8. _ ei _ _ _   —importance
9. _ eo _ _ _   —a man's name
10. _ eu _ _ _ _   —gathering of people
11. _ _ _ ia _   —10,000
12. _ ie _ _ _   —vehement, violent
13. _ _ ii _ _   —a winter sport
14. _ io _ _   —an inlet of the sea
15. _ _ iu _ _ _   —great success
16. _ oa _   —rise
17. _ oe _   —verse
18. _ oi _   —blank, empty
19. _ _ oo _   —dribble
20. _ ou _ _   —purse or bag
21. _ _ _ _ _ ua _ _   —defend
22. _ _ _ _ _ ue   —tardy, late
23. _ ui _ _   —construct
24. _ uo _ _ _ _ _ _   —citation
25. _ _ _ uu _   —a void

---

[6]"Vowel Language," adapted from "Vowel Combinations," *Saturday Review*, February 20, 1965, p. 40. "Your Literary I.Q." David M. Glixon. Copyright 1969, Saturday Review, Inc.

ELMWOOD MEDIA CENTER

Intermediate   Name_____ Class_____

WORD OF THE MONTH[7]

Fill in the blanks in the words defined on right.

Jan _ _ _ _	—doorman
_ _feb _ _ _ _	—vitality
Mar_ _ _ _ _ _	—marzipan
_ apr _ _ _	—whim
_ _ _ may _ _	—frightened
_ _ jun	—Indian
Jul _ _	—a sweet, syrupy drink
Aug _ _	—a prophet
Sept _ _	—a composition for 7 voices
_ _ oct _ _	—a teacher
_ _ nov _ _ _	—remodel
_ _ dec _ _ _ _ _	—improper

---

[7]"Word of the Month," adapted from "A Little Yearful." *Saturday Review,* March 19, 1966, p. 54. "Your Literary I.Q." David M. Glixon. Copyright 1966, Saturday Review, Inc.

ELMWOOD MEDIA CENTER

Intermediate   Name_____ Class_____

PUT IN YOUR MONEY'S WORTH[8]

You can't get rich from it, but if you put the right amount into every word in the first row you will have increased your word-treasure. Complete each word by filling in the name (some are slang words) of a monetary unit or other financial term. Synonyms and definitions of each word are on the same line in the second row.

quick _ _ _ _ _ _	—mercury
de _ _ _ _ _	—to mean
_ _ _ _ _ iose	—magnificent
_ _ _ _ _ _ _ back	—a position in football
Inde_ _ _ _ _	—improper
Pumper _ _ _ _ _ _	—dark rye bread
con _ _ _ e (slang)	—to limit
_ _ _ _ nsion	—size
_ _ _ _ _ _ able	—variable
_ _ _ _ _ age	—slavery
shoe _ _ _ _	—wading bird
_ _ _ _ _ cide	—agree
_ _ _ _ _ ty (slang)	—brave
_ _ _ _ le	—clasp
_ _ _ _ ew	—a nut

8"Put In Your Money's Worth," adapted from "Buried Treasure," *Saturday Review,* January 15, 1966. p. 70. "Your Literary I.Q." David M. Glixon. Copyright 1966, Saturday Review, Inc.

ELMWOOD MEDIA CENTER

Intermediate   Name_____ Class_____

FOR THE BIRDS[9]

Fill each blank with a bird, the name of each bird being spelled the same as the verb defined alongside (for example, swindle: rook).

1. avoid_____
2. frolic _____
3. peddle loudly _____
4. gloat_____
5. stretch forward _____
6. lose courage_____
7. complain_____
8. repeat by rote_____
9. accept without question_____
10. waver unsteadily_____
11. tilt_____
12. plunged_____
13. shoot at individuals from a hiding place_____

---

[9]"For the Birds," adapted from "Strictly Aviary." *Saturday Review,* February 1, 1969, p. 34. "Your Literary I.Q." David M. Glixon. Copyright 1969, Saturday Review, Inc.

ELMWOOD MEDIA CENTER

Intermediate   Name_____ Class_____

WHAT DO WE MEAN
and
WHERE DID WE BORROW?

Many expressions have come into our language from certain professions, games, history, superstitions, etc. Find the meaning of the expression listed below and find out where we borrowed them from. Use *Brewer's Dictionary of Phrase and Fable.*

Above board— _____

To bark up the wrong tree— _____

You're on the beam— _____

A baker's dozen— _____

Eating crow— _____

On the nose— _____

Behind the eight ball— _____

It isn't cricket— _____

ELMWOOD MEDIA CENTER

Intermediate   Name_____ Class_____

THREE IS NOT A CROWD HERE!

In all types of literature, poetry, mythology, folk and fairy tales, biography, plays, fiction and nonfiction, you'll find threesomes. Use an allusion dictionary like Benet's *Reader's Encyclopedia* and/or *Brewer's Dictionary of Phrase and Fable* to find the names of each of these threesomes.

The 3 wise men are called:_____

The 3 furies are called:_____

The 3 R's are called:_____

The 3 Jews condemned to be thrown in a furnace by Nebuchadnezzar are called:_____
The 3 fates of Greek mythology are called:_____

The 3 Brontë sisters' names were: _____

The 3 princes from Ceylon who accidentally discovered many things were called the three princes of:_____
The 3 witches in a play by Shakespeare are often called the three:

The 3 Harpies' names are:_____
The 3 Musketeers in the book by Dumas were:_____

ELMWOOD MEDIA CENTER

Intermediate   Name_____ Class_____

WHEN YOU THINK OF ONE
YOU THINK OF THE OTHER

But if you can't, you'll find it in one of the special allusion dictionaries—*The Reader's Encyclopedia; Brewer's Dictionary of Phrase and Fable.* When you find the two names that belong together do as in the example.

(5)	Mutt	1. Tyler
( )	Hansel	2. Pocahontas
( )	Tinker Bell	3. Mr. McGregor
( )	Tweedledum	4. Jill
( )	Jekyll	✗. Jeff
( )	Romeo	6. Peter Pan
( )	Sullivan, Sir Arthur S.	7. Tom Sawyer
( )	Captain John Smith	8. Gretel
( )	Peter Rabbit	9. Tweedledee
( )	Fiddle	10. Hyde
( )	Jack	11. Juliet
( )	Huck Finn	12. Gilbert
( )	Tippecanoe	13. Johnnie
( )	Frankie	14. Cat

GEOGRAPHY GAMES

It is a common complaint of many teachers that most children are weak in map skills. As a wind-up activity in a map skills unit, the class plays "Categories." The class is divided into six teams of about five children each. Each team is sent separately to the media center for exactly one half hour (a timer is used). Each child on the team has a MAPSKILLS or ATLAS sheet (pages 164-165) with him. The children help each other complete one sheet by putting their findings together in the classroom. The three teams which complete the most categories then compete against each other.

ELMWOOD MEDIA CENTER

Name_____ Class_____

Use the index or gazetteer of an Atlas, or a Geographical Dictionary to find one of each of these beginning with the letter in the box farthest to the left. Examples: in the boxes following the second L.

	CITY	COUNTRY	ISLAND	VOLCANO	MOUNTAIN
M					
A					
P					
S					
K					
I					
L					
L	London	Laos	Limnos (Greece)	Lanin (Argentina)	Lepontine Alps (Switzerland)
S					

ELMWOOD MEDIA CENTER

Find one of each of these beginning with the letter in the left-hand box, and for each find the location by longitude and latitude.

	LAKE	lat. and long.	STRAIT	lat. and long.	WATERFALL	lat. and long.	RIVER	lat. and long.
A								
T								
L								
A								
S								

Your name: _____

Your class: _____

Which reference books did you use? List them by *title*:

_____

7

Techniques and Activities for
Implementing Media Instructional
Goals Three and Four:
Children Learn to Appreciate
and Produce Media Material

Goals Three and Four are discussed together here because they develop together. They are furthered by giving assistance to teachers, directly or indirectly, by way of materials, ideas, unit outlines and often complete units with cross-media bibliographies. They include among other things helping children produce media as a presentation of their work.

APPRECIATING BOOKS

When a teacher observes that many of his students have trouble with written book reports and do not enjoy doing them, the time has come to steer them gently away from this "kill joy" to reading. For third- and fourth-year students especially, it is more fun to share books orally but it is difficult for children in this age group to organize their thoughts sufficiently to introduce a book without losing their audience. The READING CONTRACT discussed in Chapter 4, is designed for the intermediate reader. It helps children to focus on one aspect of a book for coverage in greater depth. The BOOK-TALK MEMORY CHART is aimed at an upper-level primary reader and is planned to reinforce and expand his acquaintance with the parts of a book, while making him aware of the format of books. His checked notes then serve to introduce the book. When he has finished checking the notes, his teacher briefly checks these against the book and, depending on the type of book, he selects an activity from the list below to present the book to a large or small group. He can choose:

for fiction:
1. a description of an exciting event.
2. an explanation of a favorite illustration.
3. the reading aloud of an exciting part, preceded by a summary of what led up to it.
4. the making of a diorama with a taped description.
5. to give an opinion of the book.
6. to compare it with another on the same subject.
7. to dramatize one scene, acting all the different parts.

for nonfiction: 2, 4, 6, 7 and 8
8. to explain something newly found with diagrams on the overhead if needed.

Other individualized follow-up activities to motivate further reading or investigation of the same or related topics can take many forms. Here are just a few: for a fiction book with the Netherlands as locale—find a nonfiction book on the Netherlands; locate the Netherlands on a map or in an atlas; find the exact locale of the story; look up that town in an encyclopedia—the possibilities are endless. For a book which has a bibliography in the back for further reading: check the card catalog to see how many on the list are available in the media center; if the book had a note about the author or illustrator, find out more about either or both; if you enjoyed the art work, perhaps you would like to find another book illustrated by the same artist. For a book about lizards, fascination with one type, e.g. iguanas, may lead to an exciting search for books and other materials on that beast. If two children each day get this kind of individual attention from teacher and media specialist, each child in a class of 30 will have 12 opportunities in a school year to share his reading experiences and build from them.

READING PROGRESS

Hand in hand with the BOOK-TALK MEMORY CHART (see below)goes SCORE YOUR READING PROGRESS (page 169). This is a self-evaluation sheet, intended to give a child insight into his reasons for selecting a certain book. It emphasizes that we read for different reasons; for pleasure, for information, for pictures. The more methods used to find a book the higher the score. Credit is given for trying a book that turned out to be boring, too childish or too advanced. For a final mopping up activity, the browsing puzzle IF YOU KNOW HOW TO BROWSE, YOU ARE NO SLOUCH (page 171) summarizes browsing skills in sequential order.

ELMWOOD MEDIA CENTER

Name_____ Class_____

BOOK-TALK MEMORY CHART

Author_____ Title_____

THE EVENTS IN MY BOOK:
- ____ really happened
- ____ could have happened
- ____ never could have happened

MY BOOK WAS ABOUT:
- ____ real persons
- ____ people who could have been real
- ____ fantasy characters

MY BOOK WAS:
- ____ a collection of stories by different authors
- ____ a collection of fairy and folk tales
- ____ one story divided into chapters
- ____ one story without chapters
- ____ a description of real events divided into chapters
- ____ a description of real events without chapters

MY BOOK HAD:
- ____ a foreword
- ____ a postscript or afterword
- ____ information about the author and illustrator on the jacket
- ____ information about the author and illustrator in the book
- ____ charts and/or maps
- ____ a table of contents
- ____ numbered pages
- ____ pages without numbers
- ____ an index
- ____ a dedication
- ____ a list of books for further reading (bibliography)

MY BOOK WAS:
- ____ a book of information (nonfiction)
- ____ a story book (fiction)

___ a collection of stories and poems by the same author

THE ILLUSTRATIONS WERE:

___ line drawings
___ paintings
___ photographs
___ other
___ in black and white
___ in two colors
___ in three or more colors

THE TIME OF MY BOOK WAS:

___ before my parents were born
___ before I was born
___ since I was born

THE EVENTS IN MY BOOK TOOK PLACE:

___ in the U.S.A._____
               where?
___ in another country?_____
               name?
___ on another planet
___ in an imaginary place

ELMWOOD MEDIA CENTER

Name_____ Class_____

SCORE YOUR READING PROGRESS

DID YOU FIND YOUR BOOK:

(check only one answer)
1 ___ too easy?   ( )
2 ___ too hard?   ( )
3 ___ just right?   ( )
4 ___ print too large?   ( )
5 ___ print too small?   ( )

WAS YOUR BOOK:
6 ___ enjoyable?   ( )
7 ___ boring?   ( )
8 ___ too long?   ( )
9 ___ too short?   ( )
10 ___ too childish or too advanced for you? ( )

DID YOU CHOOSE YOUR BOOK:

11 ___ because of the subject? ( )
12 ___ because it was a beautiful book? ( )
13 ___ because the title sounded interesting? ( )
14 ___ because you like the author? ( )
15 ___ because of the pictures only? ( )
16 ___ because of more than one of these reasons? ( )

TO FIND YOUR BOOK DID YOU:

17 ___ choose from a display? ( )
18 ___ select from the shelves ( )
19 ___ use the card catalog? ( )
20 ___ ask for help from the media
        specialist? ( )
21 ___ ask a friend? ( )
22 ___ use more than one of these
        methods? ( )
        How many? ( )

DID YOU:

23 ___ read the whole
        book? ( )
24 ___ read certain parts you
        were interested in?
        ( )

DID YOU:

25 ___ read only the paragraphs
        (captions) under the pic-
        tures? ( )
26 ___ look only at pictures? ( )

Put a ✔ on the lines after the numbers for the best answer(s) to each question. When you have done all 26, look below to find out what your score is.

  Very Good: 25   Satisfactory: 14-20

You need to improve your method of book selection if your score is under 14.

SCORE: 1(0); 2(0); 3(5); 4(0); 5(0); 6(5); 7(2); 8(0); 9(2); 10(2);
11–21 (1 each); 22 (the number you put in the parentheses); 23(3); 24(3); 25(3); 26(3), only if you got 1 point
for 15 also.)

ELMWOOD MEDIA CENTER

Name_____ Class_____

IF YOU KNOW HOW TO BROWSE
YOU ARE NO SLOUCH

1. When you sample,
   Try out, you are b_ _ _ _ _ _ _
   You must be awake,
   Alert, not drowsing.
2. When you come to the library
   For specific

   1⊅4 {Welcome} 2000 ₭ꞵ *i* , *lbs.*

   You won't have time for
   For this favorite occupation.
3. In the library do often
   ⌐≈ꞵse in new places.

   Your best-loved book friends
   Were once unfamiliar f _ _ _ s.
4. If you look a book over
   Within and without,
   Don't forget to look
   On the flap of the j_ _ _ _ _,
   You'll get an idea
   What it will be about
   You'll know should you take it
   Or chuck it.

5. If you admire the pictures by the
   s o r l u t a r t i l,
   It will be no surprise to you
   That the story is even greater.
6. Another way of telling
   If a book is for you,
   Is to look at its size
   And its _ _ i _ _.
   If a book is fat,
   Often its letters are _ _ _ _ _.
   When you take it home
   Will you read it all?
7. When the *B⌀t* M *6* are bigger
   And the book is s _ _ _ _ _ y,
   You'll need less vigor
   'Cause you're reading a mini.
8. Did the bvuips write to you?
   Look in the front of your book.
   You may find a special message
   For the little trouble you took.

9. Reading this message is like a game
   It'll add to your reading pleasure.
   Its content is never quite the same:
   This message has three different names:
   _ o _ _ _ o _ _; p _ _ _ _ _ _, or _ _ _ _ _ _ _ _ _ _ on
   Don't skip it; read it for good measure.
10. You found a groovy book,
    Now you want another.
    Look in the card catalog
    For a second one by this 26. 6. 7. 19. 12. 9.
11. In alphabet order it is aligned,
    In _ on _ _ _ _ _ o _ books only, in back.
    It is very handy if you want to find
    On a certain subject, information you lack.   Answer: _ _ _ _ _
12. How to d t q y u g intelligently
    Is what you here did learn.
    Now follow this method diligently
    And great rewards you'll earn.

A language arts unit seasoned with media for upper-level primary children covers a mixed bag of skills and appreciations. Interpreting titles, understanding plot, getting an insight into authorship and an appreciation of originality through creative writing, are combined with editing, proofreading, reading aloud, handling A-V equipment and using the card catalog. The unit's title, *Book Brothers,* refers to its eventual outcome: a comparison between a published book and children's picture-book interpretations of the same title. It is most easily done with small groups of five or six at one time. As an activity it can continue until everyone in the classroom has participated or, if desired, year round. At the rate of half an hour daily, a three-week period is needed for each group.

A collection of attractive and suitable picture books or, better yet, their jackets is borrowed from the media center. New or unfamiliar books are best. The first meeting of the group is with the media specialist. The children speculate by examining the covers and titles what the books might be about. During the discussion it is brought out that people are attracted to books by interesting titles and eye-catching book covers. They will soon reveal if they have read one of the books. For a book that interests him but he has not read, each child orally suggests a plot, on the basis of the title and the jacket illustrations. He writes it down in one paragraph or less.

Now the teacher takes over. Each child's plot outline is developed further during language arts and eventually becomes a picture story in book form, or in any audio-visual format it lends itself to. *Book Brothers* can easily be adapted to the different needs and abilities of children by concentrating only on one or two of the most necessary skills for some and covering a greater range with others. Opportunities for individualization present themselves during the daily writing and editing process; able spellers can be paired with poor ones during proofreading; creative artists but poor writers with good writers; verbal children with nonverbal ones.

A-V PRESENTATION

When the stories are completed, the authors and illustrators—as many as three children can collaborate successfully on one story—singly or in groups present their productions. Many use a tape recorder combined with an opaque or overhead projector. A slide show with taped narration, produced by using an instamatic camera to photograph scenes staged with dolls and stuffed toy animals or other props, is an interesting possibility and good training for future film making. A stick- or hand-puppet show is always successful and easier when the narration has been taped beforehand.

After each story is presented, its namesake is read to the class by the teacher. A discussion follows which focuses on: the aptness of the title for each story; the problem (plot) in each story; and the originality of the ideas in the stories. As an exciting finale letters written to the authors of the namesakes, enclosing thermofax copies of the *Book Brothers,* could result in interesting correspondence. Searching the card catalog for other books by the authors will yield more good reading. Asking children to select two small books on the same subject by different authors for comparison will promote further understanding and appreciation of each author's individual contribution.

MAKE A PRODUCTION OUT OF IT!

Make a production out of it consists of 10 classroom-tested recipes for book productions to take the place of tedious oral and written reports, presented for the reader's choice.

IMPERSONATIONS. Impersonate one of the people in the book and tell, on tape, what happened to him, or to another important character.

"HOW TO" DEMONSTRATION. Make something from a "how to" book. Then demonstrate to the class exactly how to make it. It could be a recipe, a science experiment, the organization of a collection, a crafted object.

SHARE WHAT'S NEW. Share one or more newly learned things with the class. Explain it on the overhead projector, using a transparency. Present the class with a diagram to show what interested you; for example: the way a turtle fits into his shell. Ask the class if they can tell what it is. If they can, it is a good and clear presentation.

COMMERCIAL, SINGING OR NOT. Advertise a book by making a singing or straight commercial

in prose or verse. Illustrate on the overhead if desired.

DID YOU SEE THE MOVIE? Compare a book with its movie
version.

SELL IT TO T.V.   Present a book as a soap opera or situa-
tion-comedy T.V. show with interrup-
tions for commercials and all.

IT'S TRANSPARENT! Select the most important event in a
book and tell or tape what happened;
illustrate on overhead.

LOOK THROUGH CHALK TALK. Tape a book talk and
illustrate it with stick figures on the
overhead as the tape is played.

KEEP THEM GUESSING. Introduce the book characters with
stick puppets and act out the events
which lead to the climax or the problem
of the book, while playing a prerecorded
tape of these events. Then stop the show
and ask the audience to solve the problem, in a buzz-session. Compare the
group's endings with the way the author
solved the problem.

SING, RIDDLE AND RHYME. Record the plot of a book as a
song, riddle in verse or poem about the
book. Set to existing or original music, if
possible.

These book productions are all geared to intermediate children.
The tape recorder is heavily used because it is a marvelous tool to
help children overcome shyness, and the stumbling block of writing.
Making a production of it creates awareness and appreciation of
media, their possibilities and limitations, by comparing them and
translating one into another. Sequential presentation requires skill in
organization and facility with a variety of A-V equipment, singly and
in combination. Some examples of riddle poems by children which
were made into book-marks for distribution in the media center
follow.

ART-MEDIA CORRELATION

The Lively Art of Picture Books, a Weston Woods film, was
the inspiration for the art unit which is described here. A child who
is exposed to a carefully chosen collection of picture books, films

Book Riddle

This house in five books
Was cooky and spooky
In winter it was hid
'Cause the river had ice.

About a portrait on
the wall,
Old grandmother knows all.
You'll like these books
to the end,

They will become
Your friends

by Jill Gradner

Answer: The Children of Green Knowe

Book Riddle

A witch and a friend
Until the end.
Winter snow was nice
Once they walked
Bare foot on ice.

Until a spell....
A soft heart;

The friendship
will fall apart...

... But not for long,

It's on again,
This time it's not
pretend.

by Jana Warren

Answer: Jennifer Hecate, Macbeth, William McKinley and Me, Elizabeth.

Book Riddle

Once there was a little house

Long ago and far away

The children worked
In the morning
And played in the day.

They lived in the woods
And made their own goods.

by Jill Gradner

Answer: Little House In the Big Woods

Book Riddle

Brought home in a hatbox,
All cramped and asleep,
Lay the grey haired animal
Who caused such a heap
Of trouble, laughter, mischief
and more.

Whose mistress found out
He wasn't a bore.
The problem was now
To keep him... but how?
Hilarious?... You bet!
What a funny thing
To have for a pet!

by Jana Warren

Answer: Julie's Secret Sloth.

Clue: This pet hangs up-
side down from a
tree branch.

A Valentine to an
author I love.

Hearts and flowers
To Beverly Cleary,
Who gave me hours
That were never dreary.

When I had adventures
With Henry and Otis,
Time was passing
And I didn't notice.

Have you read about
Ribsy,
And Beezus, that past?
Tell me which book
You liked the best.

Into a poem shape it
If it's good we'll tape it.
It does not have to rhyme
But it must have reason
To win a prize
This Valentine Season.

MHW

On a boat, there is
A baseball team,
With a female coach
Beyond reproach.

She did not scream
When bases were loaded
And the batter struck out:
She just exploded!

When it came to the
championship
She did not keep a
clamp on her lip

When the choice was
Between honor and winning
Her love for truth
Won the inning

This is a Valentine
To a Jewish Mother,
Who was a good sport
Like her, there's no other!

MHW

Read: The B'Nai Bagels
by Konigsburg

Valentine to an Author

Again you have done it
Dear Mrs. Gannett.

You made me wiggle
Laugh and giggle,
When the crocodiles
Smiled their crooked
smiles.

Your pictures are so
funny,
They make my eyes go
funny,
They show every little
thing

That make your stories
interesting.

When you Bum Crack
from Tangerine,
Will you become
My Valentine?

MHW

Read: My Father's Dragon
by Gannett

To a Book I love:

Her father was a king
With many jewels and
rings

He sailed the ocean blue
As captain with a crew.

She had a monkey
and a horse,
They were her friends
of course.

She was happy every-
where

And as strong as a
bear!

poem by
laurie
woolf

Read:
Pippi Longstocking

and filmstrips which have been made of the cream of the picture book world, consciously or unconsciously deepens his experience of the world around him, as he perceives it through the eyes of many different artists. Such a collection is in effect a viable art collection with which he has more intimate contact than he could have with any museum collection. This art resource becomes the basis of a unit in art covering work in a number of art media. The children gain insight into how artists communicate, and become aware of style and authenticity. In passing, children become familiar with illustrator cards in the card catalog. They'll meet a local author-illustrator in person and other author-illustrators on film. The unit touches on authorship and book making in preparation for a later experience: the creation of a simple picture book for very young children. The unit is intended for fifth- and sixth-year students.

The art teacher begins by showing *The Lively Art of Picture Books* up through the part where it is explained and shown how differently various well-known illustrators depict trees, cats, and other familiar subjects. The film is stopped here and a discussion follows about how individual and original each artist's perception of the same subject is. The term "style" is introduced and the meaning of style explored. Examples of style in fashion, building, way of living, writing, individual sports (tennis, golf, swimming) are solicited from the children. As a follow-up the children are asked to find two picture books by the same illustrator in the media center and compare them in terms of the artist's style, with emphasis on originality and relationship of the subject to the style.

In the lessons that follow the art teacher first discusses various art techniques and media such as line drawing with pen and ink, charcoal and pencil, watercolor with brush or wash, painting, lithography in black and white and color, wood and linoleum cutting, engraving and photography. The children follow up in the media center by finding out what the process of each technique consists of. They find examples in books in the media center.

When the class meets again the teacher uses the examples the children have found to project with the opaque projector for purposes of further clarification. Children's art work using different techniques and media are also used to demonstrate the same purpose.

During the next few meetings the children work on rendering a specific subject, the same for all, in various media with a variety of techniques. The results are grouped by the media used, except for one group which includes one piece of work in each of the media used. The work is displayed in these groupings. A discussion on the ways in which the children used the different media and techniques to express the same subject follows and is focused on two questions: Is one medium or technique more suitable for the subject than another? and, is the style of an artist affected by the technique or medium he used?

To conclude, the children choose two picture books, illustrated by different illustrators from the list below and complete a brief BOOK-ART CRITIQUE (page 179) for each.

Alcorn, John
Ardizzone, Edward
Aulaire, Ingri d'
Bemelmans, Ludwig
Brooke, Leslie
Brown, Marcia
Caldecott, Randolph
Charlip, Remy
Cooney, Barbara
Crane, Walter
Daugherty, James
Domanska, Janina
Dubois, W. Pene
Emberly, Ed

Fisher, Leonard E.
Gag, Wanda
Greenaway, Kate
Hogrogian, Nonny
Hurd, Clement
Katzoff, Sy
Lamorisse, Albert
Lawson, Robert
Lenski, Lois
Lionni, Leo
McCloskey, Robert
Montresor, Beni
Munari, Bruno
Piatti, Celestino

Politi, Leo
Potter, Beatrix
Rackham, Arthur
Raskin, Ellen
Rojankovsky, Feodor
Sendak, Maurice
Shepard, Ernest H.
Spier, Peter
Steig, William
Tensen, Ruth M.
Tudor, Tasha
Yashima, Taro
Wildsmith, Brian
Zemach, Margot

Intermediate   ELMWOOD MEDIA CENTER

Name_____ Class____

BOOK-ART CRITIQUE

Illustrator_____

Title_____

Underline the type of illustrations you found; if you found more than one type, underline those used:

photographs in color; black and white
single line drawings
wood cuts
lithographs in color; black and white
paintings
watercolors
collages

Did the illustrator work in:

realistic style; simplified style; imaginative style; cartoon style

Did he use authentic details? _____yes _____no
If you checked yes, list some:_____
_____

If your answer is no, can you give a reason?_____
_____

Underline what you think and explain if the illustrations are:
interesting; amusing; different:_____

Do you think the medium and technique are well suited to the subject? yes __ no __ Explain why_____

Can you think of another medium or technique that would be good for this book?_____
_____

CHILDREN BECOME AUTHORS

Again for fifth- and sixth-year students, *Young Books By Young Authors* follows smoothly on the trail blazed by *The Lively Art of Picture Books*. A part of the language arts program, it covers creative writing, simple plot construction, the use of a thesaurus to find interesting descriptive language, and the writing of simple verses with the use of a rhyming dictionary if necessary.

A collection of picture books, chosen this time primarily for their good plots or original treatment and format, are borrowed from the media center. Short and concise books are the best examples. The teacher brings them in and asks a group of children to display them attractively in the room, without telling them what they are for. Deliberately he does not take notice of them for a few days and puts off children who ask questions. At last he engages the class in a guessing game as to their use. They may come up with some ideas better than this one. If so, he develops a unit around one or more and shelves this one; but if everything goes according to plan, he shows the film *The Story of a Book,*[1] "which follows a real life author, H. C. Holling, through the exciting and satisfying progress of creating *Pagoo,* the story of a hermit crab. . . ." It also shows how author and illustrator work together closely in observing and record- ing the habits of the captured hermit crabs, so that their story, though imaginative, will be based on facts about the life cycle of hermit crabs.

Once the film is shown, the reason for the presence of the picture books in the room becomes clear: the children are going to write their own, for very young children. The class is given a twofold assignment during the following two weeks: to read as many picture books as possible with special attention paid to the subjects the books are about and the authors' use of words. They are also assigned to observe a small child at play and take notes on his interests and behavior. (Does he talk while playing, sing, make up games, pretend?) From the books and the notes a list of themes and interests on which books might be written for small children and the ways of authors with words is put on the board. This list might read as follows:

---

1. The *Story of a Book* is available *free* from the Special Services Section, Film Library, Library Extension Division, New York State Library, Albany, New York, for all libraries in New York State.

THEMES AND INTERESTS	WAYS WITH WORDS
Animals	Rhyme
Family	Words in different size
Children, like themselves	letters
Holidays	Nonsense
Seasons	Sentences carried onto
Pretend friends	next page
Nature	Picture clues
Birthdays	Repetition
Toys	Counting
Being afraid	Good descriptions
Being shy	Words that imitate sounds

They begin to write, incorporating these observations into their stories, after returning the picture-book collection to the media center (to prevent plagiarism). During the procedure of writing, it is fun to try to duplicate as closely as possible what goes on in a publishing house, as shown in the film *The Story of a Book*. While the teacher remains editor in chief, the appointment of copy editors (proofreaders) and associate editors to work with small groups of authors creates a small-group learning situation. The group of copy editors can edit the books of the associate editors, and vice versa. Individualization takes place when the editor-in-chief confers with each child about cutting, taking care that story line flows well and discussing final format and placement of illustrations and word choice. *Roget's Thesaurus* is used to find words to express an idea—a synonym dictionary to find just the right word.

When books are completed appointments are made to read them to kindergartners. Books may also be produced audio-visually.

Another art-related activity is an Egg Tree with prizes for the 10 best eggs, which goes up before the Spring Recess. This gives children a chance to decorate their eggs during the vacation. A reading of *The Egg Tree* by Katherine Milhous and *The Whiskers of Ho-Ho* by William Littlefield presented over the school intercom as a radio program to the primary grades familiarizes the children with the world-wide folk custom of decorating Easter eggs. The intermediate children are invited to research egg-lore around the world, and the participants together stage a radio program for broadcasting on the last day before the vacation. Two weeks after the Spring Recess prizes are awarded for the 10 best eggs, in the following categories:

1. the most original

2. the most beautiful
3. the most carefully done
4. the best dressed
5. the funniest
6. the best animal egg
7. the most artistic
8. the best traditional Easter egg
9. the most imaginative
10. the coolest egg.

Names of winners are always posted in the media center on the pertinent bulletin board, and also announced on the intercom. For most contests that originate in the media center, there is a small reward or prize. Miniature Mars Bars or Milky Ways are very much sought after. Many children want to know in advance what the prize will be; often they decide which contest to enter by the prize offered!

FOR REMEDIAL PURPOSES AND INDIVIDUALIZATION

One-to-One Read-In is a program for intermediate children who are reading below level. It is a cooperative venture of the remedial reading teacher (or the reading teacher), the kindergarten teachers and the media specialist. The remedial reading teacher and the media specialist together decide in advance which books are most suitable for each child and select up to five titles for each. A SPECIAL READING RECIPE sheet (see below) is then typed up for each child who wants to participate. Participation is on a voluntary basis, but before long everyone wants to read to a kindergarten child. During reading time two children a day come to the media center with their SPECIAL READING RECIPE. They locate one of the books on the recipe and take it back to their room to prepare to read it aloud. Preparation includes: knowing the meaning of all the words; correct pronunciation and enunciation, reading without stumbling and with expression.

When a child has satisfactorily prepared his book he may go to the kindergarten and select a friend to read it to. The kindergarten teachers have prepared their class for this event. When the older children pick up a kindergartner of their choice, they take him to the media center and select a quiet corner to settle down. At first they generally choose a child they know but the kindergarten teachers see to it that everyone gets a turn. After reading to their charges they

Special Reading Recipe
for: _____
Cooked up by your Book-Cook

teach them how to borrow the book, if they wish to take it back to the classroom. If not, they help the kindergartner choose another book to check out and take to the classroom. In this way kindergartners become accustomed to borrowing procedures before their official initiation to the media center. As a special treat, when a child's reading has shown some improvement he is allowed to present a picture book in filmstrip format to a whole class of kindergartners.

ENRICHMENT THROUGH MYTHS

Mythallure and Legendry is a unit which lends spice to the study of ancient civilizations or the modern countries in those areas where myths and legends originated. Incorporated in the language arts program, vocabulary work with words derived from the myths and legends follows logically. Creative writing of original myths and poetry; the understanding of allusions; oral reading of myths onto tape and listening to gather information; mapping the geographical locations of the myths; puzzle activities; all are designed to make intensive use of the media center and its resources.

Why study myths and legends in this modern day and age? Myths and legends, the first dramatic works of literature, open the eyes of our sophisticated, science-oriented children to the imaginary and delightful ways in which the ancients interpreted the natural world. They will begin to see that our culture bears the stamp of mythology in many places such as speech, laws and customs. Our language and thinking are full of ideas and words derived from mythological and legendary sources. Some familiarity with these sources will be helpful in later years for an understanding of the great epic poems of English literature and poetry in general.

Any of the three puzzle activities: CLASSICAL CLASSIFIEDS, WHO IS THE OTHER HALF and MYTH CROSSWORDS (pages 187-189) or all three, will get the unit off the ground. These activities create interest and will motivate children to choose a mythological or legendary character to read about. After preparing it at home, groups of children read their myth onto tape for the whole class to listen to. In this way a collection of myths on tape becomes available for everyone to share by listening.

The children concentrate on the following questions while listening (they may take notes if they want to):

Were the gods all powerful?
How were they like men?

Did they get along with each other?
How did the gods show their goodness or anger to man?
How do myths explain certain natural phenomena?
How are heroes different from gods?

When through discussion of these questions the children understand that the power of the gods was limited and that they had weaknesses and squabbled among themselves, they will understand that the gods were created by man in his own image. From the ways in which gods punished man and for what, they will perhaps see that human pride was particularly offensive to the gods. As most children will not readily understand the symbolism of the myths which explain natural phenomena, an explanation of one of them (for example the myth of Demeter, the earth mother, and her daughter Persephone or Ceres, the goddess of agriculture, whose departure for the underworld for six months explains the Greek winter) will open the door to understanding others. How heroes differ from gods is best experienced by a serial reading of the *Odyssey,* chronologically, in the media center.

A number of projects for small groups and individuals include:

Plotting the locations of mythological and legendary places on a map of the area in which the legends originated

Making a scrapbook of pictures and symbols cut from periodical advertisements and using mythical symbolism and names or words, explaining each entry's mythological origin (example: Atlas tires—strong tires named after Atlas who carried the world on his shoulders)

Preparing a family tree of the gods

Finding a myth which explains the name of a heavenly body or constellation

Making a dictionary of words and sayings derived from myths

Finding jokes or cartoons in periodicals for which a knowledge of mythology, legend or folklore is required to get the point. Making overhead transparencies of them and stumping the class.

Dramatizing a myth, legend or folktale

Finding songs and poems about characters in myths legends or folktales

Making a short rhyme or poem about a mythological character, pretending you are he or she, for example:

If I were Pan, my pipe I'd play
For maid and man the livelong day,
I'd rock and roll the whole night long
with young and old and weak and strong.

Writing an original myth explaining how a local or imaginary animal, bird, rock, flower, mountain, river or other landmark got its name.

Making a list of gods and their symbols or implements

Making masks (art correlation) representing mythical characters and pantomiming the myths while a narrator, live or on tape, tells the story.

Intermediate   ELMWOOD MEDIA CENTER

Name_____Class_____

CLASSICAL CLASSIFIEDS [2]

Pretend that these classified ads appeared in a newspaper in ancient Greece. Can you find out which mythical characters (numbered at the bottom of the page) placed the ads? When you match the advertisers to their ads, place their numbers in the parentheses in each ad.

HELP WANTED

BIRD CATCHER needed to kill ravenous bird, attacking helpless victim daily. No one afraid of heights should apply.
Box ( )

TECHNICIAN needed to construct a prison maze. Contact isl. king.   Box ( )

SITUATIONS WANTED

BULLFIGHTER, boar-hunter, presently unemployed. Will consider underground assignments, kidnapping, etc. Box ( )

CHARIOT DRIVER, inexperienced, eager. Days only. Will try anything once.   Box ( )

MUSICIAN, vocal and instrumental. Wide experience. Good with animals. Will travel.
Box ( )

STRONG MAN, hard worker. Clean stables, trap wild animals, odd jobs. References.   Box ( )

EQUIPMENT WANTED

ADVENTURER on dangerous mission needs highly polished shield. Will return after use.
Box ( )

TEEN-AGE FLYER needs a new flight pattern, wing repair kit, life preserver. Urgent.
Box ( )

LOST AND FOUND

LOST: PRECIOUS FRUIT. Return to garden, or forward information concerning thief to Sisters, Far West.   Box ( )

LOST: WATCHDOG, ferocious, unusual appearance. Fond of cake, music. Write Tartarus, Main Gate.   Box ( )

FOR SALE

BED, used. We fit all sizes.
Box ( )

FINE SHROUD, hand woven, unfinished but exquisite workmanship.   Box ( )

[2] "Classical Classifieds." *Saturday Review.* Feb. 15, 1969, p. 42, "Your Literary I.Q." David M. Glixon. Copyright 1969, Saturday Review, Inc.

(for sale)

GRAPES by the bunch or ton. Quality wines. Write: Master of the Revels.   Box ( )

OPPORTUNITIES

GUIDED TOUR. 10 year cruise with shrewd captain. Mediterra-

(opportunities)

nean area; some land excursions. Route subject to change.
                Box ( )

YOUR FUTURE accurately foretold; life spans our spe- cialty. Always three in atten- dance.   Box ( )

1. Dionysus; 2. The Fates; 3. Hades; 4. Hercules; 5. The Hesperides; 6. Icarus; 7. Minos; 8. Odysseus; 9. Orpheus; 10. Penelope; 11. Perseus; 12. Phaëton; 13. Procrustes; 14. Prometheus; 15. Theseus.

ELMWOOD MEDIA CENTER

Intermediate   Name_____ Class_____

WHO IS THE OTHER HALF?

In myths, legends, and Bible stories there exist many stories of inseparable friends or relatives who are usually referred to in one breath. Here is a list of one of each pair. Find his (her) other half!

FIRST HALF	OTHER HALF
Adam----------	
Daphnis-------	
Cupid----------	
Pyramus------	
Isis -------------	
Philemon-----	
Echo-----------	
David ---------	
Pythias -------	
Cain------------	
Romulus-----	
Daedalus-----	
Castor---------	
Gog-------------	
Patroclus-----	

ELMWOOD MEDIA CENTER

Name_____Class_____

MYTH CROSSWORDS[3]

Identify the following characters from mythology, whose initials will spell from top to bottom:

1. The Hindu god of the dead: Y _____
2. The supreme Scandinavian god: O _____
3. The father of the Titans: U _____
4. The sun god of ancient Egypt: R _____
5. The mother of Castor and Pol-
   lux: L _____
6. High flier and son of Daedalus,
   who took a dive when his
   wax melted: I _____
7. Latin name of the god of wine: B _____
8. Twin brother of Romulus: R _____
9. A Titan who felt the world's
   burden: A _____
10. Popular incarnation of Vishnu
    and hero of great Hindu epic: R _____
11. The giant from whose body the
    Scandinavian gods created
    the world: Y _____
12. The daughter of Agamemnon.
    She was almost sacrificed to
    the gods, before the Greeks
    sailed for Troy: I _____
13. The other name of Romulus,
    the legendary founder of
    Rome: Q _____

---

[3] "Myth Crosswords," adapted from "Mythacrostic," *Saturday Review,* July 27, 1968, "Your Literary I.Q." David M. Glixon, Copyright 1968, Saturday Review, Inc.

ENRICHMENT THROUGH FOLKLORE

Incorporating folklore and folksongs in this unit is accomplished easily by adding THE MESSY TOOLSHED (page 191) and SING-IN (page 192) to the list of puzzle activities. The music teacher might enjoy working with this song puzzle which is intended to familiarize children with first line indexes of song books. Additional folksong puzzles are easily devised by using first line indexes of a variety of song collections.

ENRICHMENT THROUGH NURSERY RHYMES

A folklore unit centered around Mother Goose rhymes is popular with everyone from the second through fifth and even sixth year. The suggestions for activities in this unit are adaptable to whatever level is desired, so *Let Them Loose On Mother Goose!* During the course of the unit the children will become acquainted with the lesser known Mother Goose rhymes; they will learn to use first line indexes in Mother Goose collections as well as poetry books and poetry indexes; they will be doing dictionary work with obsolete meanings of words; penmanship is included as well as creative writing of original new Mother Goose type rhymes.

The children will discover that Mother Goose collections and other collections of rhymes and verses, including almanacs and books of days, are a goldmine of entertaining riddles, warnings, proverbs, predictions, prescriptions, game songs, wise sayings, charms and spells, and old-fashioned commercials in the form of street vendors' cries.

This unit may be included in the language arts program as part of the poetry program or in the social studies program, when studying France, Great Britain or the United States. Mother Goose rhymes may be scrutinized to find customs of the past—the American Mother Goose collections compared to the English. Weather rhymes may be singled out and investigated as weather lore with a science unit on the weather. Finding expressions we use today which came from Mother Goose is another possibility. Creating cracked Mother Goose rhymes and modern Mother Goose riddles to hang in the media center, lettered on large pieces of attractively lettered colored construction paper, signed by the creator, is happiness!

One way to begin the unit is by collecting television commercials

ELMWOOD MEDIA CENTER

Intermediate   Name_____   Class_____

THE MESSY TOOLSHED

A great deal of information can be found on a catalog card, if you read the fine print. If the answer can't be found on the card, locate the book itself and look it up there.

See if you can find the tool that belongs to each of the characters in the left column. They got awfully mixed up in the right-hand column. After the owner's name write the letter of his (her) tool in the parentheses. The first one is done as an example.

Gib Morgan	(*i*)	a. sledge hammer
Mike Fink	( )	b. knife
Zeus	( )	c. whistle
Paul Bunyan	( )	d. powder horn
Jim Bowie	( )	e. long pole
Rumpelstiltskin	( )	f. broom
John Henry	( )	g. lasso
Casey Jones	( )	h. spinning wheel
John Chapman	( )	✗ oil rig
Cinderella	( )	j. axe
Pecos Bill	( )	k. cooking pot
Davy Crockett	( )	l. trident
Neptune	( )	m. lightning bolt

ELMWOOD MEDIA CENTER

Intermediate   Name_____ Class_____

SING-IN[4]

In these lines from ballads, popular songs, folk songs, and poems please answer each question with the right name, word, or phrase. (No singing aloud!) Choose the right phrase from the bottom of the page.*

1. I've got a mule, her name is Sal—/Fifteen miles on *what?*

_____

2. *Whose* wife is a young thing and cannot leave her mother?

_____

3. Oh, bury me not on the lone prairie/ In a narrow grave, just *how big?* _____

4. *What* ran a hundred years to a day?_____

5. (*Who?*) pulled out her big forty-four/ and the gun went rooty-toot-toot.

_____

6. I'm (*who?*)/ I feed my horse on corn and beans._____

7. And for (*whom?*) I'd lay me down and dee._____

8. Goodbye, (*who?*)—I'm a-leavin' Chey-enne._____

9. (*Who?*) was a railroad man—/He worked from 6 till 5._____

10. (*Who?*) is the best sailor/ That sails upon the sea.

11. In a cavern dwelt a miner/ and his daughter, (*who?*)_____

*old horse-shay; Annie Laurie; Sir Patrick Spence; Billy Boy; 6 x 3; Ol' Paint; The Erie Canal; Frankie; Clementine; John Henry; Capt. Jinks of the Horse-Marines

---

[4] "Sing-In," adapted from "Songfest," *Saturday Review,* February 22, 1969. "Your Literary I.Q." David M. Glixon. Copyright 1969, Saturday Review, Inc.

in rhyme and asking the children to write some of their own. As you read them slip in a Mother Goose street cry, for example:

Hot cross buns, hot cross buns/One a penny, two a penny/Hot cross buns,/If your daughters do not like them/Give them to your sons.

This ploy usually works to send the class hunting for other Mother Goose commercials. Another method is to listen for jump rope or other game songs or formulas the children chant on the playground. Jot one down and ask the class to make a collection of current game jingles. Compare these to Mother Goose rhymes and when some in each category have been written down, start a classroom display called *Mother Goose Is On the Loose* or *Mother Goose Is Making News* or whatever title is catchy and collect Mother Goose rhymes in many categories. On the bulletin board find one example for each category and put it up as an example in penmanship. Have the children write their finds in their best writing, and build lessons in penmanship around the copying of the verses they have located in the media center. The following examples will start each category in style:

MOTHER GOOSE THE WEATHER MAN

If Candlemas day be fair and bright
Winter will have another flight,
But if it be dark with clouds or rain
Winter is gone and will not come again.

P.S. What prediction do we have today for the same date?

ALMANAC NEWS FROM MOTHER GOOSE

Plant pumpkin seeds in May
And they will run away;
Plant pumpkin seeds in June
And they will come up soon.

P.S. Can you find a verse for every month of the year?

YOUR HOROSCOPE BY MOTHER GOOSE

Who is born on Easter morn
Will never know want, care or harm.

GUESS, SAYS MOTHER GOOSE

Riddle me, riddle me, what is that,
Over the head and under the hat.

MOTHER GOOSE VALENTINES

If you love me, love me true,
Send me a ribbon and let it be blue;
If you hate me, let it be seen,
Send me a ribbon, a ribbon of green.

MOTHER GOOSE GAMES FOR GENTS AND DAMES

Pease porridge hot, pease porridge cold,
Pease porridge in the pot, nine days old.
Some like it hot, some like it cold,
Some like it in the pot, nine days old. (clapping game)

LULLABIES FOR BABYSITTERS, WITH COMPLIMENTS FROM MOTHER GOOSE

Hush my baby, do not cry,
Papa is coming by and by;
When he comes, he'll come in a gig
Hi cockalorum, jig, jig, jig.

CHARMS AND SPELLS TO GIVE YOU MOTHER GOOSE PIMPLES

Laugh before it's light
You'll cry before it's night.

Ash tree, ashen tree,
Pray buy this wart of me.

MOTHER GOOSE ADVISES THE LOVELORN

If you find a hair pin,
Stick it in your shoe;
The next boy you talk with
Is sure to marry you.

With these examples as guides the class organizes in small groups. Each group chooses a heading to work on, in the media center. They come as groups and go through the table of contents of Mother Goose and poetry collections. They also use an index to children's poetry. The media specialist teaches how, on an individual basis.

Penmanship exercise and improvement is incorporated in the copying of the verses for the bulletin board. The teacher works individually with children and in small groups with those who need the same penmanship exercises.

The whole class votes on a favorite verse in each category to produce as bookmarks, to be designed during art class. Bookmarks executed in India ink or pencil can be produced in quantity on the Thermofax copier for distribution to all pupils through the media center.

The meaning of old-fashioned words such as tarry, Candlemas and gig may be included in vocabulary work by older children; it will introduce them to the organization of the unabridged dictionaries.

MOTHER GOOSE HUNT (page 198) is a puzzle activity to follow up on the use of first line indexes; best for intermediate children. MOTHER GOOSE IS CRACKING UP (page 199) is a contest for the best fractured Mother Goose rhymes. Some which were entered at Elmwood Media Center follow:

There was an old woman
Who lived in a shoe,
She had so many children
She didn't know what to do,
So she moved!

Little Jack Horner
Sat in a corner
Eating his Christmas pie;
He put in his thumb
And pulled out an apple
And said: "Oops, the wrong pie!"

Jack and Jill went up the hill
To fetch a pail of wine;
Jill fell down
And broke her crown
And Jack got the hiccups.

Little Bo-Peep,
Go blow the clarinet;
It is easier than the horn.

Mary had a little lamb
With fleas as white as snow;
Everywhere that Mary went
That scratching lamb would go.

Hickory dickory dock,
The mouse ran up the clock;
The clock struck two—
Oh dear, I'm late.

Hey diddle diddle,
The cat and the fiddle
The cow jumped over the moon
And went into orbit.

Jack was nimble,
Jack was quick,
Jack ate the candlestick
And got heartburn.

Jack and Jill went up the hill
To fetch a pail of water;
Jill fell down
And broke her crown
And said: "Oy! weh is mir!"
(Elmwood School has a large
Jewish population)

Hickory dickory dock,
The mouse ran up the clock;
The clock struck one,
The mouse had fun
Until he got an electric shock.

Marry, Mary quite contrary
How does your garden grow?
Well, we had too much rain.

Jack was nimble, Jack was quick
Jack jumped over the candlestick
And burned his . . . .?

Humpty Dumpty sat on the wall,
Humpty Dumpty had a great
   fall;
And all the king's horses
And all the king's men
Had scrambled eggs.

London Bridge is falling down,
Falling down, falling down,
Good . . . one less bridge to cross.

A surprise reading experience for little ones is unintentionally packaged in MOTHER GOOSE IS CRACKING UP. The large attractively lettered and frequently illustrated rhymes were fun to read all around the dropped ceiling frieze of the media center. The surprise endings stopped young readers short, but only for a moment. Curiosity was high and most children did not give up until they had figured out the endings. Because the rhymes were put up as they were composed, there were always new ones to decipher. A total of 32 verses were contributed by children from the fourth through sixth years.

Primary children particularly enjoy Mother Goose riddles. It is not hard for them to locate these in Mother Goose collections by using the table of contents which is often organized by subject. After stumping their classmates with the Mother Goose riddles they have located, it is not too difficult to make up some riddles in rhyme of their own. A collection of common household objects brought into school, such as buttons, kitchen utensils, a zipper, beads, a top, are placed on a tray and children take them to their seat, handle them, and observe them for their unique characteristics. For example, a button sometimes has two holes, sometimes four and sometimes a stem with a hole. A zipper has teeth, a pair of scissors, legs and eyes; when it is open it forms an X:

Of eyes I have four
And sometimes two;
I help you close
Your coat for you.

        suoʇʇnq

When I bite my teeth
I keep you warm;
No winter winds
Will do you harm.

        ɹǝddᴉz ɐ

MUSIC CORRELATION

As music correlation the music teacher might like to introduce the children to the "Mother Goose Suite" by Ravel. The finding of Mother Goose songs in song collections and on recordings is another possibility. Children who have created Mother Goose riddles could write music for them and record them on tape. A new mod Mother Goose Suite written by the children from their songs is another idea.

It was mentioned before that understanding and appreciation of media is the result of using them, enjoying them, comparing them and—very important—producing them, no matter how primitively. To produce media of any kind a child must be able to translate one experience into another and give it a new form. In so doing he adds a new dimension to his thinking and learning processes which gives him insight and allows him to conceptualize through association of ideas.

FILM PRODUCTION

Examples of media produced by children were given before under Goals III and IV in this chapter and in Chapter 4, where the possibilities of producing tapes, filmstrips, transtrips, (filmstrips on acetate) photographic slides, or combinations of these were discussed. The more often a child has had any of these production experiences, the more ready he will be to undertake the making of a short three minute cartridge film in his fifth or sixth year.

Making a film is an exciting creative activity and is an ideal complement to creative writing in the language arts program. It may seem formidable and very technical but it is not, if working with the right equipment. With a super 8mm camera which has an electric eye (a built-in light meter), automatic focusing and a single frame exposure control for animation, it is not necessary to be an expert photographer or cameraman. It is of course nice to have a model which can be synchronized with a cassette tape recorder to make sound films eventually, but at first it is really better to make silent films, because the problem of getting the message across without sound creates greater awareness of the limitations and possibilities of film as a medium. If desired, separate soundtracks can be taped and played simultaneously with the film. Floodlights and a tripod are a must.

Using the equipment itself is the easiest part of film making; it

MOTHER GOOSE HUNT

   Use a first line index in any large Mother Goose collection to find the next two or three missing lines of the Mother Goose rhymes below:

Peter White will never go right;
Would you know the reason
   why?

_____

_____

***

As I was going to sell my eggs,
I met a man with bandy legs,

_____

***

Little Robin Red Breast,
Sitting on a pole,

_____

***

There was an old woman
Lived under a hill

_____

***

What's the news of the day,
Good neighbor, I pray?

_____

_____

***

Johnny Armstrong killed a calf,
Peter Henderson got half,

_____

_____

Mirror, mirror tell me,
Am I pretty or plain?

_____

***

Hector Protector was dressed
   all in green,
Hector Protector was sent to the
   the queen;

_____

_____

***

Lucy Locket lost her pocket,
Kitty Fisher found it,

_____

_____

***

Barney Bodkin broke his nose,
Without feet we can't have toes;

_____

_____

***

Alas, alas for Miss McKay,
Her knives and forks have run
   away

_____

***

Cackle, cackle, Mother Goose,
Have you any feathers loose?

_____

_____

_____

_____

Intermediate   ELMWOOD MEDIA CENTER

Name_____
Class_____

MOTHER GOOSE IS CRACKING UP

You can tell that Mother Goose is cracking up by the kooky endings on her rhymes. Now that she is cracking up anyway, why not help her along a little bit? If you don't know the rhymes below, look up the last few lines which have been left off and make up a silly one in their place, as in the examples below:

Wee Willie Winkie runs through
  the town,
Upstairs and downstairs in his
  nightgown;
You would think his mother
  would buy him some pajamas!

Peter, Peter, pumpkin eater,
Had a wife and could not keep
  her

Jack Sprat could eat no fat,
His wife could eat no lean

Little Tom Tucker
Sings for his supper

Bat, bat, come under my hat
And I'll give you a piece of bacon

Twinkle, twinkle, little star,
How I wonder what you are

Pussy cat, pussy cat, where have
  you been?
I've been to London to look at
  the queen

Ba ba, blacksheep,
Have you any wool?
No sir, no sir,
Only dacron today.

Three little kittens
Lost their mittens

It's raining, it's pouring
The old man is snoring

See saw, Margery Daw,
Sold her bed and lay in the
  straw

Willie Willie Wilkin
Kissed the maids a' milking

Fiddledeedee, fiddledeedee,
The fly shall marry the
bumblebee

Old King Cole
Was a merry old soul

boils down to reading the directions carefully, making a trial film using a variety of techniques and locations, and not being afraid of making mistakes. Teaching children how to translate what they want to say into the film medium is harder. It can be done effectively by showing them inductively how films come about, by giving them problem-solving, sequential experiences with various media before the actual filming. The film-making process is broken down into its essential steps and becomes an adventure in planning, sequencing, and logical thinking, as well as an art experience. For imaginative films the work is best done in small groups as a language arts activity. For films which express curriculum content, teachers generally take the time from the allotment devoted to that subject matter and allow the children to meet with the media specialist for this purpose in the media center.

At first the children are made aware of the fact that making a film is expressing an idea, not in words but in pictures. To illustrate that one medium can be translated into another, they are given different rhythm instruments and large pieces of paper and crayons. They make sounds with the instruments. Each child then expresses the sound of his instrument on paper by drawing a picture of the sound. In turn each child then tells why he made the picture light, dark, warm, cool, full, empty, squiggily or straight, etc. Next they are asked to think of a smell they like or dislike. Again they translate the smell into a picture. By looking at each other's pictures, the children try to infer from the drawings whether the smell was a good or a bad one. Musical clues may be given by accompanying the drawing on an appropriate rhythm instrument.

The second activity is interpreting silent film loops and writing a brief script for them. Film loops which they have not seen before are borrowed for this purpose. All children see the same one first and write a script for it. The scripts are taped and compared, and the best one becomes a permanent addition to the media center collection. This exercise sharpens the children's observation and again they are translating one medium into another.

Next, films made by other children are obtained and critically viewed. They are all shown without sound. The techniques used in these films are discussed and explained. It becomes apparent that live actors are not needed to make films. Some of the children understand that objects can be used in films as symbols for people.

Finally a group of sound films on values is shown.[5] These films are planned to invite audience participation by being open-ended. A moral problem is posed in each of them and there are no right or wrong answers. They are first shown without sound and the group tries to interpret them and figure out what the problem is. To confirm their interpretations, or correct them, the films are shown again with sound. When the group members are able to do this without too much error, they show that they understand that a film maker must prepare his audience for what is coming; that he must focus the viewer's attention on what he wants him to see. This understanding grows from discussion of the clues as viewed in the silent version of the film.

Now the group is ready to begin its own films. When the children have formulated an idea they want to translate into film, and it may be as simple as "flowers are beautiful" or as complicated as "landing on Mars," they put a brief plot outline on paper or on tape. The next step is the planning of a story board for their film. In about 16-24 frames they will draw sequential sketches of the action, beginning with a title frame. As each child finishes he creates the background for the various scenes (which may be done as an art correlation) and the characters he will use as actors. These may be clay figures, dolls, puppets, apples, bananas, flowers, paper cut-outs, real people, real animals—whatever strikes his fancy. When all props and scenery are ready and set up in the A-V production room, he may spend a few hours, on consecutive days, filming with the assistance of the media specialist, who at this time initiates him in the intricacies of camera handling and otherwise acts as assistant to the director. The finished film is processed commercially and not edited, mainly because it is too time-consuming and requires special equipment.

In spite of careful story-board planning technical and sequence problems do come up during the filming. To show that an astronaut in his spaceship was approaching Mars, a child solved this problem during the actual filming, by replacing the construction-paper planet with Marses of ever increasing size, each showing greater detail during the filming of an animated movie of a landing on Mars. When film runs out too soon, endings have to be scrapped and changed

---

5. *The Clubhouse Boat, Trick or Treat,* and *Paper Drive* produced by Dimension Films, 1969;   adapted from Fannie R. Shaftel and George Shaftel,   *Role Playing for Social Values,* Prentice- Hall, 1967, and distributed by Churchill Films, were the films used.

drastically, or action inferred rather than shown to save footage. Accomplishment is so satisfying however (and pretty immediate too; it takes less than a week to develop the film) that these problems are challenges and not frustrations. Making films with elementary school children is not as formidable an undertaking as it may seem, but it certainly is a formidable learning experience.

8

The Appropriate Use and Misuse
of Audio-Visual Equipment [1]

New teacher or old, you are a sophisticated old hand at using the many marvels of the TV age—the A-V stuff. You've used the tape recorder, the phonograph, the filmstrip projector, the sound projector and many more. They are an integral part of your thinking and your classroom planning. Great; how about taking a new look at the A-V world? How about deliberately planning to misuse all your versatile and exciting A-V machines? Game? Read on.

THE 16mm PROJECTOR

Let's look first at the standard 16mm projector. This is a useful tool. The teacher finds a film, on a topic of study. She threads it, focuses, lets the film run to conclusion, stops the machine, leads a class discussion, makes a note as to its value for next class, or next year, and is finished (after rewinding, of course). This goes on daily in thousands of classrooms across the country. Why? When one watches a movie, or a show on TV, one expects to be shown a full-length production without stops. After all, the screen is only a place for the spectator to focus his vision. But, you control the machine in your classroom, not a projectionist or an engineer. You can make it a useful tool. You can be a magician and in so doing

[1] Adapted from "The Deliberate and Appropriate Misuse of Audio-Visual Equipment" by Glogau and Krause; *Grade Teacher* Magazine, Jan. 1970 (with permission of the publisher). Copyright 1970, by CCM Professional Magazines, Inc. All rights reserved.

enhance your instructional program. How? Try some of the following suggestions:

1. Take any short film on any topic and show it to your class without sound. Direct the children to read lips or to figure out what is happening by watching other visual clues. (Begin the film after the title.) In the ensuing discussion, the children will share their observations. Then, replay the film with the sound on. This is a very useful technique to encourage children to observe carefully. It might also make them sensitive to the problems of people afflicted with hearing loss.

2. Play parts of a film in reverse with or without sound. You might want to reverse the procedure which shows a scientific experiment. It is useful to reverse sequences which show physical movement of people to point up grace or coordination. Many humorous effects can be produced by showing events in reverse with sound—like an explosion falling back on itself, or a speaker with broad gesticulations. Reversing action is also a means of motivating children for creative writing. A reversal is actually a going-back in time—a finding the beginning of the action.

3. To help children develop the idea of a sequence to events, it is useful to select only part of a film to be shown. The class would then discuss where they thought this sequence might occur in the complete film. This is useful in science films as well as in dramatizations of events such as in social studies, guidance, English.

4. Children love to solve problems where they have an opportunity to be a detective. This activity will enthuse and excite students. Separate the class into three or more groups. Select a complete sequence from a film and show each group a small section of that sequence. One group will be shown no part of the sequence. This is the detective group. It will confront the members of the other groups who will remain silent unless called upon to answer. The questions it asks will help the detective group determine what happened in the sequence. All of the groups will be involved in listening to the answers because no one knows what the complete sequence actually was—having seen only a small part of it. When a solution is reached and shared, replay the entire sequence so that all may see it.

5. In foreign language classes you might want to try the following activity which will help children develop language facility and fluency. Show a sequence of any film without the sound. Ask the children to prepare a narrative for the sequence in the language they are studying. Replay the sequence while the child or children narrate. For another activity, the teacher, a child, or a group of children might preview a short film and tape record a foreign language narrative which would be played as an accompaniment to the film while the class sees it. The original sound track would not be played.

6. For art, dramatics, or creative writing, the following demonstration might be useful. Play all or part of the soundtrack without projecting the picture. Direct the class either to act out the soundtrack, draw a sequence of pictures to accompany it, or, in the case where only part of the soundtrack is played, write the next sequence or the conclusion.

OVERHEAD PROJECTOR

The overhead projector is coming into wide use in many parts of the country. Transparencies are being manufactured for it by the thousands. Many of them have two or three overlays; some of them move or create the feeling of motion by the use of color, variously grained surfaces, and a polarizing device; all of them add excitement to the classroom by adding depth to the instructional program. The teacher, by means of a grease pencil or felt marking pens, is able to write on a sheet of clear plastic as on the old chalkboard with the added advantage of having her words, diagrams, or examples projected above and behind her and magnified to the point where everybody in the class can see it; and she doesn't have to turn her back on the class. All of these uses are fine, but they, by themselves, tend to limit the applications of this most useful tool. Try some of the following suggestions:

1. Because it projects silhouettes so well, the overhead projector is an excellent tool for providing primary school children with concepts of groups of things like fives, fours, twos, etc. Any size coins or other materials may be used for this purpose. You can even use colored plastic discs which are translucent and which look very pretty when magnified and projected. Cuisinaire rods can be demonstrated in terms of their relative sizes by use of the overhead projector.

2. The overhead projector is a fine replacement for the old flannel board. Fractional parts, geometric planes and shapes, geometric parts arranged to form shapes of animals and so on, can all be used and enhanced through this instrument.

3. Because of its bright light and fine lens, the overhead projector can be the sole property for producing shadow plays with children and/or puppets.

4. Fine transparency maps can be projected to almost any size and traced when deemed useful for class purposes. A whole wall can be used to map a state or a country or even a neighborhood block in very large scale.

5. The relative size, as a concept for any age child, can be demonstrated through the use of the overhead projector. Flat objects, either in silhouette or drawn on clear plastic, can be projected to almost any size for easy comparison.

6. By rigging mirrors at an angle above the stage in a school auditorium, one can use the overhead projector as a scene projector. Whatever setting is desired is drawn and colored on a regular transparency sheet. It is then projected onto the mirror above the stage. The mirror is angled so it will reflect the scene on the backdrop. The actors then go about their business in front of the backdrop. This saves the time, energy, and materials that go into making scenic backdrops.

7. Psychedelic effects can be created by placing wheels of multi-colored cellophane on the projector platform and rotating them slowly. It is possible that some child may mechanize this device by means of a battery-operated small electric motor. This can be used for school art classes as a type of mobile sculpture, or at school dances, or as an environmental effect for poetry reciting or story reading.

8. For a trip through time and history, rig up a transparency of a famous man or woman and put on a small overlay that simulates mouth movement or movement of other facial features. Project the picture on the wall at a magnification which would make it appear lifesize, and have a child hold discourse with it. The mouth or features would move as it responded.

TAPE RECORDER

This useful and versatile machine has confounded many teachers because it has more than one knob or switch to operate. Also, a great many people shun it because they are either "mike" shy or they are afraid they will erase the deathless pronouncements on the tapes. But children do have to develop aural and oral discrimination as well as visual discrimination. Many manfacturers who are aware of the potential time-saving uses of this device are putting whole programs on tape including directions for the students. Some creative teachers are doing the same. Try some of the following suggestions:

1. Prepare all spelling or dictation tests on tape with normal time for response allowed. This could be for a group or for the class. The teacher is then free to work with other groups or to walk around the class as she desires.

2. Use it to play back or record all or parts of a lesson, speech, or debate.

3. Use it as a self-improvement device. It is useful for developing pronunciation, proper tone and modulation, appropriate speed, volume and pitch. Recording the way you speak during a lesson will help you grow. It does the same for children who then learn to listen to themselves as they really sound.

4. It is a great device for helping children develop inflection when reading and reciting. Children become more aware of the uses of punctuation marks and pauses when they read or recite before a group.

5. Many actors use this as a rehearsal device. They either record all of the parts and listen to them over and over, or they record their own part and the cues preceding their lines, or they record all parts but theirs and leave appropriate gaps for their lines which they speak to the machine. Many actors use all three techniques. Children might use it this way as well. It is a spur to memory.

6. Many children do not observe well with their ears. They do not possess good sound clues to their environment. A teacher might walk through a neighborhood from which her pupils come and record all of those ongoing daily and familiar sounds like a garbage truck, a dry cleaning store, a bus stopping or starting, the sound of a mailbox opening and closing, etc. By learning to identify sounds, children become more aware of their environment.

7. The teacher might record sounds of different places: the country, the city, the department store, the super market, the

office building, the subway, etc. These, again would help children develop useful discrimination.

8. A useful, interesting, and fun activity is to ask children to try to spell sounds much as the comic books printed the sounds of fights with words like bash, sock, splat, slap. Other words like rrrinng produced the sound of a bell ringing. This activity helps children develop letter-sound discrimination as well as helping them become more fluent with words.

9. The teacher might record a sequence of sounds either from life or from sound-effects records. She would play this sequence and ask the children to develop a story from the sounds which would follow the sequence in which they heard them. Such a sequence might have the following sounds: car screeching to a stop; running footsteps; doorbell or knocking sound; opening and closing door sound; sound of an elevator; etc.

10. A good tape recorder with a monitor switch can be used in a very practical way with its microphone attached. It serves as a reasonably good PA system in assemblies, at sports activities, or at dances.

FILMSTRIP AND/OR SLIDE PROJECTOR

This relatively inexpensive device is probably found in more classrooms than any of the other equipment. There are thousands of filmstrips available in every subject area from many, many sources. In order to give this tool a different dimension, many manufacturers of filmstrips are now producing narrations on records or tapes to accompany them. In order to accommodate these advances, many filmstrip machines are built with a record player attached.

For years this machine has been used as a see-and-read device. The strip would be shown, one frame at a time, while various class members would laboriously read the affixed captions. Some strips of thirty or more frames would put an entire class in a somnolent state by the time they were concluded. This would so dilute the educational effects of the material that whole classes would groan when the teacher would announce that it was time to view a filmstrip. Some of the following suggestions should prove useful:

1. Preview a filmstrip first. Show only a frame or two, or only as many frames as are necessary to demonstrate the point that

must be made. Show only a frame or two each day if this will serve the purpose of the unit.

2. Turn the film so that the caption does not show. Have the children narrate their own caption.

3. Get transparency paper and mount it as slides. It is then possible to have children draw their own slides or strip films to illustrate a lesson or a report.

4. For art, it is possible to teach animation techniques through the drawing of simple stick figures in slightly different poses on a series of transparent slides.

5. You can use an overhead projector, a filmstrip projector and a camera together to make animated filmstrips. This is a sophisticated procedure which can be lots of fun. Create colorful backgrounds which will be projected on a suitable surface by the overhead projector. Draw the characters on slides changing the movement slightly on each slide. Project the slide figure on the overhead projection background and take a picture of each projection with a 16mm film camera. When the film is developed, show it through the 16mm classroom projector.

6. Show a film and ask the class to write a point-by-point summary of it. Each point agreed to by the class would be illustrated by a class member as a frame for a slide summary of the film. Photograph the illustrations with a 35mm or a 126 instamatic camera using slide film. Members of the class would then tape record a narrative to accompany the slides. These slides could be shown to other classes or to small groups of students wanting information on that topic. A fine and useful slide library can thus be added to the school's media center.

7. The filmstrip can be used as a review or testing device. Certain frames can be shown and the class instructed to write or comment on the salient features of each frame.

The suggestions offered in this chapter have been tried somewhere by some creative classroom teacher. In the trying they have enhanced the learning process for thousands of students. They have also offered wide latitude for the use of equipment and material which has only been narrowly appreciated. They take film watching out of the realm of busy-work and relate it to learning in a dynamic manner. Through these appropriate and deliberate misuses, the potential of the media center is continually expanded.

MEDIA CENTER AIDES AND OTHER TEACHER HELPERS

We hope that your school will budget for the employment of media aides. These valuable personnel will enhance the use and presentation of A-V material to an extent far beyond their cost. They will assist the media specialist, of course, but their help to the teacher will be far more rewarding. Essentially, they will be responsible for setting up equipment for use either in the center or in the classroom. They will respond to the teacher's need for a particular piece of hardware and the particular material to use with it. The aide will set up the film to run forwards or backwards. He will also prepare transparencies, tape recordings, and the like for classroom use and presentation. His most valuable additional function will be to train children in the use of the media and its hardware, as well as his assistance in the training of teachers. If the media aide's work is confined exclusively to the media center, then he would train the para-professionals who work in the classrooms to perform the necessary functions relating to classroom use of all A-V media. Where it is not possible for the school to afford the expense of media aides immediately, the media specialist should train teachers in the use of A-V equipment. It is especially useful when several staff members have expertise in this area.

9

Simple, Practical Remodeling Plans
for Your Present Library

SHORTCOMINGS OF THE PRESENT SCHOOL LIBRARY

If we accept the limitations of previous school architecture, we are doomed to continue the patterns of education they impose. Most older school buildings, even many of those built within the last decade, have been constructed on the self-contained classroom philosophy. It has been difficult to break away from this pattern of little, teacher-run fiefdoms even with the current barrage of changing ideas about learning and teaching. Most frustrating to many educators have been the limitations of the present school library. No child would ever mistake it for any other room in any building. In most cases, it can be described as a one-room book repository—a hollow sound-box with four walls of shelving surrounding long or circular tables at which students sit silently, studying, writing, or reading. The librarian, for all his training, acts mainly as a book clerk and occasionally teaches the Dewey Decimal System. The room contains few, if any, nonbook media; storage space is small or nonexistent. The librarian may have a desk and a filing cabinet for his own materials, but there is usually no library office, nor are there any facilities where audio-visual material can be stored or produced. To add further to this already sad picture, the library is usually heavily scheduled. This allows children time to take out or return books, and it structures and limits the times when they might research a report. Rather than becoming a place for excitement, discovery, or serendipity, the school library in this setting is a drab place, lacking in ambiance; a place where a student has to go, not one to which he wants to go. The media center concept can revitalize your present school library. If a teaching staff accepts its potential, it can alter the nature of the educational program. Let's examine some possibilities.

INEXPENSIVE ARRANGEMENTS FOR A ONE-ROOM MEDIA CENTER CORE FROM YOUR PRESENT LIBRARY

Ideally, the media center should be the physical as well as the philosophical heart of the building. It should be surrounded by learning areas, small and large group instruction areas, independent study areas, and discussion areas. Students should have access to it many times each day. The ideal is not always possible, however, so let's redesign your present library to make it function as the core of a media center.

We will assume that your present library is at least one room and that it is accessible to the student body in its present location. Hopefully, there are adjacent classrooms, or offices, or closets which may be incorporated at some later date into an expanded media center. For now, a simple rearrangement of the materials already in your library can help you to get started.

Prepare a layout of your present library by setting the room to scale on graph paper. Using the same scale and construction paper, cut out rectangles, squares, circles corresponding to your present shelves and furniture. (It doesn't matter if your present shelves are fixed to the wall, they can be removed.) Now is the time for fun! Decide how you want the space broken up and then involve the staff in moving the construction paper furniture and shelves within the outline of your present layout. You will find that it is more useful to remove the shelves from the wall and use them as stacks.

Plates 9-1 and 9-2 are illustrations of the same elementary school library before and after it was redesigned.

The following suggestions are listed for your convenience. Some have been used in Plate 9-2.

1. Set up a picture book area in one corner of the room, surrounded by shelves, and carpeted so children can sit on the floor for browsing or story telling.
2. In lieu of an office, which is desirable, set up stacks of reference material surrounding an area where you will put your desk and other equipment.
3. For variety, put some of the tables between the stacks rather than in the center of the floor.

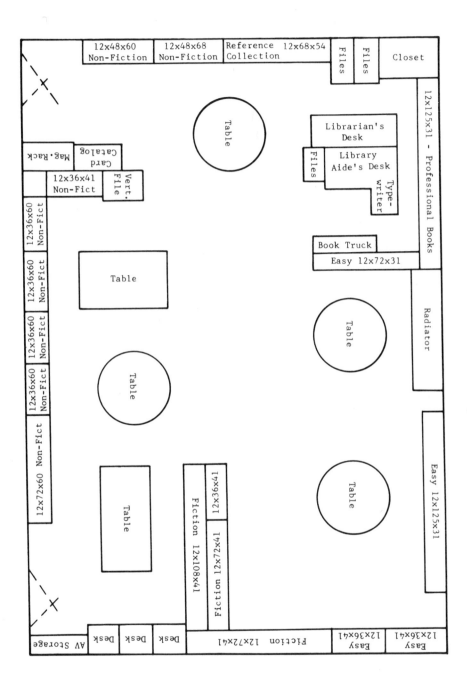

Plate 9-1

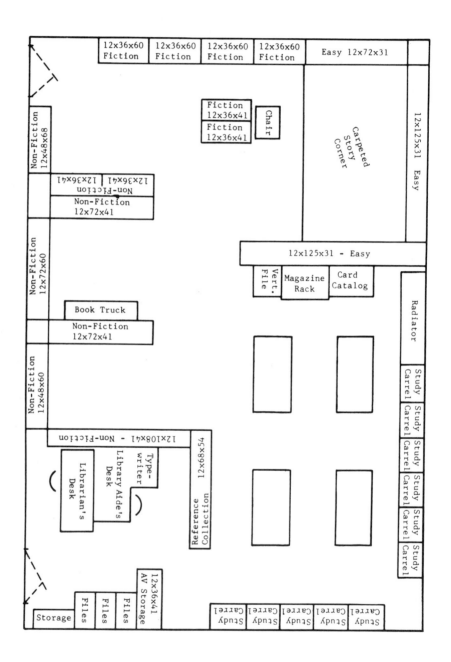

Plate 9-2

4. Build plywood partitions which are portable. These are inexpensive. When used on a standard library table, circular or rectangular, these can be fitted together to make separate study areas for four to six children.
5. Convert your round tables to listening centers by placing appropriate hardware in the center of the table with earphones placed around the circumference. For individual listening, portable plywood partitions will convert the table into study areas for four children.
6. Why not eliminate tables?! Replace them with individual carrels made up of old desks with plywood sides and backs nailed on. These desks can be arranged in any grouping you desire. Outlet boxes can be added to allow children to use the carrels for viewing filmstrips, listening to record players, or tape recorders, etc.
7. Go ahead—eliminate furniture altogether! Carpet the floors instead. Buy or make cushions, preferably flat, for sitting on. Stock 2'x3' masonite boards on which students would do their writing, while sitting, kneeling, or lying on the floor. Places against the wall can be used for filmstrip viewing and/or other A-V explorations.
8. Portable carrels, (three pieces of ½" plywood, each 2'x2', hinged together) should be made available for students who want to avoid distraction.
9. Purchase small bicycle baskets, or small canvas covered metal frame baskets which can be stored against the walls between the stacks. Students who are using media for research can store their materials in the baskets between visits to the center. A nametag on the basket will identify its owner. (This is based on children having access to the media center at least once daily.)
10. Rethink your ideas about lighting in your media center. Light can vary from one place to another depending upon its need. While strong light is desirable for the stacks and study areas, it is not necessary in the listening or viewing areas. Purchase floor and desk lamps, or have them donated. Place them around the reading and study area for student use.
11. Place inexpensive foam-cushioned arm chairs at the corners of the stacks to provide for recreational reading. Place floor-lamps in these areas.
12. Make room near the fiction stacks for small discussion groups.

Furnish this area with a foam couch and some chairs. Place some lamps in this area for additional light.

13. Painting is a must! This must be among the first considerations for redesigning. It adds immeasurably to the new environment you want to create.

SUMMARY AND SOME COST ESTIMATES FOR ONE-ROOM MEDIA CENTERS

Any combination of the above suggestions will alter the approaches and use of your present library room. To create a media center environment, you first have to break step with traditional library ideas such as the hollow-box plan for books and tables. Items #1, 2, and 3 offer the least expensive conversion. All they require is your time and labor in rearranging the shelves into stacks and then fitting your tables and chairs into the new order. Item #4 requires less than $50 to build portable plywood partitions for placement on rectangular tables to serve the needs of over 30 children. The partitions are slotted thusly (see below) and fit into each other to allow for six children at a rectangular table. For the same amount you could add plywood sides and backs to old desks to make individual carrels for 16 children. This includes a 1"x10" pine shelf for book storage on each carrel. Outlet boxes can be added to each desk for a very little more. This takes care of item #6.

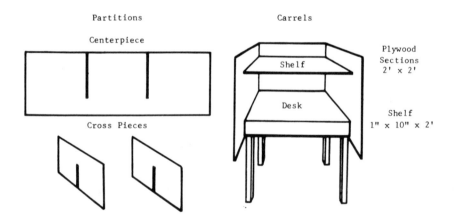

Item #7—Carpeting the center costs about $1 per square foot; but this can alter the center in a drastic manner. It cuts down on noise dramatically. It also makes possible a reduction in the need for furniture. Most students will prefer to work directly on the carpet using masonite boards for writing purposes. These boards are cut from 4'x6' or 4'x8' quarter-inch masonite sheets at a cost of $4 to $6 per sheet. Vinyl or heavy cloth-covered cushions cost $2 to $4 each. The portable carrels in item #8 should cost from $2 to $3 each. The baskets in item #9 should cost about the same. The "Better Light–Better Sight" lamps which are relatively free from glare cost from $14 to $25 depending on whether you want desk or floor lamps. You could furnish a one-room media center for under $100 as suggested in item #10. The couches and armchairs mentioned in items #11 and #12 are priced at about $50 per chair and $75 to $100 per couch. Six chairs and one couch will cost less than $400. For the average elementary school of 600 children, that's less than 75¢ per child.

In developing your plans and budget, you might decide to carpet one area and buy lamps, chairs, and a couch for the rest of the media center–all for the cost of what carpeting alone might have cost.

Rather than building portable carrels or partitions (or in addition to, if you like), you can purchase earmuffs (that's right! earmuffs!) and provide them to children who are easily distracted by noises.

The above suggestions make it possible for you to redesign your present library into a media center core at relatively little expense.

SOME INEXPENSIVE IDEAS WHERE THERE IS LITTLE ROOM FOR STORAGE

Where curriculum needs have to be met and where nonfiction books and ancillary media are in short supply, teachers can rotate their teaching of various units. The media specialist can help this situation by purchasing rolling carts–one for each curriculum unit in social studies, for example. Each of these carts is then loaded with all materials, A-V included, which are pertinent to the unit. These carts can be displayed as centers of attraction in the media center and then sent to the classes which require them for their unit work. However used, these carts offer a solution to the lack of shelving which would be a problem in the expanded uses of a one-room media center.

Putting all pertinent media together on the same shelves is also a very useful idea. Robert Muller, writing in the *School Library Journal* (2/70), states:

> Physical separation of learning materials is an antique idea, and is not compatible with the concept of the media library. Integration is the keynote, and is essential to the promotion of a cross-media

learning. Ideally, all kinds of media on a single subject should be kept together, if not on the same shelf, then at least in the same area.

The media specialist should be constantly on the lookout for all kinds of containers of various sizes so that tapes, records, filmstrips, transparencies, *and* books can be stored together or adjacently.

If the media center is not large enough to have carrels where hardware for viewing or listening can be placed, then the outside corridor might be used for this purpose. Attach a folding shelf to the wall outside of the library. This shelf can be 20 feet in length to provide room for ten children, or there can be five four-foot lengths set up next to one another. These shelves would fold down when not in use. The school electrician can install outlets or an outlet strip in the wall under the shelf, so when the shelf is folded down it covers the outlet. When a child desires to use some A-V equipment, he takes it and a portable plywood separator which the media specialist gives him. He then sits in the hallway at a portable carrel and watches, listens, or both, with the material he is using. Hallway lighting is not bright; but brightness is not critical for this activity.

REDESIGN USING AN ADJACENT ROOM

If you are lucky enough to have a connecting room available, you can think about designing a very different kind of media center. One room could have the stacks for fiction and nonfiction materials; the other would have individual study carrels, listening centers, small group instruction or seminar areas, and the office which would have room for the media specialist's materials as well as a work area for the production of media—transparencies, filmstrips, ditto masters, tape recordings, etc. Here the media specialist, her aide, or both, would work to provide for teacher and pupil needs. It would be possible to allow teachers to work here, too. The costs are not high for this conversion. Extra wiring would have to be provided to take care of the additional needs of media and A-V hardware. A wall would have to be removed wholly or in part and another wall or two would have to be constructed for the office and workroom combination. One wall of the office would need a large window from which the media specialist or her aide could supervise the area. Folding screens or an accordion door or two could be installed to create small group instruction or seminar areas. Let us examine an attempt by one school, the Joyce Road School in Plainview, New York, to expand its media facility when an adjacent room became available. The following plans, specifications and cost estimates were submitted to the Board of Education for consideration. (Plate 9-3 shows the layout of the library as it then existed; Plate 9-4 shows the layout of the adjacent connecting room.)

SPECIAL PROJECT: MEDIA CENTER–JOYCE ROAD SCHOOL

I. DESIRABILITY AND NEED FOR THE PROJECT

For the past two years and for the foreseeable future Joyce Road is an intermediate school. This fact has great instructional implications. The instructional needs of intermediate grade children center around process goals. This necessitates that students be constantly exposed to media of all sorts. These media, aside from standard books and reference materials, must include filmstrips, film loops, records, tapes, transparencies, posters, pictures, maps, and the audio-visual equipment necessary to project, record, or play them. There must also be an area where students can use these materials, and furniture which will permit them to work individually or in small groups.

II. PROCEDURES PLANNED

Joyce Road will soon have twenty-one (21) classes instead of the twenty-two (22) it now has. Future projections indicate that this figure will be constant. This will enable us to free the room next to the present library for use as the research and resource room of our media center. The room presently has a connection to the library by means of a door through the wall. Certain modifications will need to be made to prepare the resource room and to change certain elements in the present library:

1. A 3 x 5 foot pane of glass in the wall next to the present door connection to enable the librarian, the library aide, or the teacher to look into either room for visual supervision.
2. Approximately 900 feet of pine shelving (1" x 12") to accommodate the book storage needs of the new resource room.
3. A wall partition built in the new room to section off space for an office-workroom. This partition wall will have a 3 x 8 pane of clear plastic which would permit a view of the students from inside the office-workroom. The office-

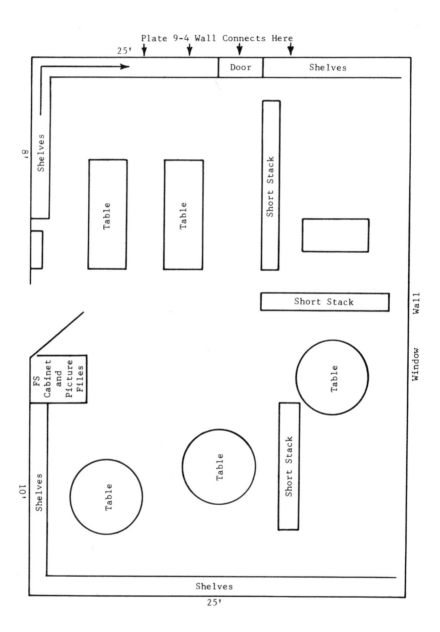

Plate 9-3

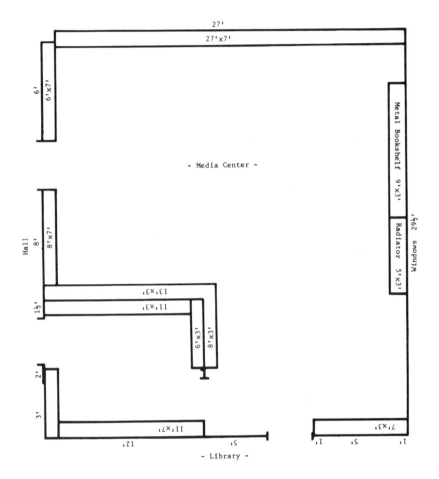

Plate 9-4

workroom will also have a door with a glass pane for entrance from or into the resource room. Since the area planned for the office-workroom was formerly an office, there is presently a door opening into it from the corridor.

4. There will be six (6) double outlets placed in the floor for the convenience of students using A-V equipment at their carrels.

5. Twenty-four (24) 28'' desks from our current supply will be modified to be individual study carrels. Each carrel will have an electrical outlet built in and a shelf.

6. A table. for the use of six to eight children will be set up with appropriate A-V equipment to be used as a listening center.

7. Forty (40) chairs will be ordered to use at carrels, listening center, and for general library seating to supplement those we have at present.

8. Four (4) tables will be ordered to provide proper seating places for those using the entire media center.

9. Various filing cabinets, card catalogs, filmstrip cabinets, and appropriate furniture will be ordered to supplement our present furniture.

10. Various A-V equipment will be ordered specially for use in the media center.

11. The library as a two-room media center will need the services of a full-time aide.

12. Acoustical carpeting of the type used in public libraries and theaters will enhance the environment of the media center.

With the inclusion of the aforementioned furniture, materials and personnel, the media center will begin to be a proper place to both initiate instruction and provide a laboratory for achieving the process goals.

III. ESTIMATED COSTS

1. 3' x 5' pane of glass $ 40.00
2. Shelving: 1" x 12" pine painted to resemble oak;
   900 ft. at $.25 per linear foot
   plus 25 sheets of 4' x 8' backing at
   $4.80 per sheet—

            Lumber— $225.00

            Backing— <u>120.00</u>

                          345.00

3. Office-workroom: partition w/ 3' x 8'
            plastic pane and door w/ glass pane   200.00
4. Six (6) double-outlets in floor @ $15 per outlet   90.00
5. a. Lumber for making side and back panels on
       28" desks for use as study carrels
       ¾" plywood—9 sheets of 4' x 8' @ $10   90.00
   b. 24 8" x 24" shelves of ¾" plywood—
       1 sheet of 4' x 8' @ $10   10.00
   c. Electrical outlet in each desk @ $5 per outlet   120.00

6. Carpeting for both rooms	1940.00
7. Library aide (full time)—an additional	1400.00
	$4235.00

8. *Books and reference materials—*

The American Library Association standards as of February 1969 will set 3% of the average per pupil expenditures as a minimum to be spent each year for library books, and an additional 3% to be spent on A-V materials and A-V equipment. The State allocation per pupil is presently $760; 3% amounts to $22.80 per pupil for library books, with an additional $22.80 for A-V materials and equipment.

The school library media center has great need for a wide variety of materials. It is also the central resource for our individualized reading programs which require continual pupil exposure to great numbers of books. There is also a need for ever larger amounts of resource and supplementary books and pamphlets to enhance the research skill training of the intermediate student.

The previous A.L.A. standard was that $4 to $6 per pupil be spent on library books and the same amounts be spent on A-V materials and equipment. A quick survey of previous budgets shows that we have been permitted to spend far less than that. The district objectives require that we eventually reach and even top the A.L.A. and/or State suggested minimum expenditures for library books. We request that additional funds be allocated for these expenditures.

9. *Priorities for the Media Center—*

We realize that some of the materials we have requested for the media center are beyond the scope of the funds provided in any annual budget without the aid of a grant. The following items are those we consider to be basic for setting up the center.

1. 3' x 5' pane of glass	$ 40.00
2. Shelving	345.00
3. Office-workroom	200.00
4. Six double-outlets	90.00

5. Lumber for making carrels—and sheets   a.   90.00
   of plywood for shelves   b.   10.00
                                                 $775.00

    Although Joyce Road School obtained the additional room for its use, the board was unable to find any money for its conversion the first year. The administrators of the school, working closely with the librarian and the building's A-V expert—a classroom teacher with expertise in that area—designed the connecting room for the use of students as a study area. Some rectangular tables were found and moved in with folding chairs for seating. Transparencies and other A-V materials were also moved into the room as were the reference books. This freed the other library room for mostly fiction use, with room for browsers, and for story telling. These activities could take place without interfering with the reference room use and allowed for a wider latitude in scheduling for the entire school.

    However, better things were in store for Joyce Road School. Two classrooms, one of which had a glassed-in office attached, had previously had one connecting wall removed and replaced by an accordion folding wall. This wall was opened from time to time to permit team teaching with two or more classes, or large group instruction and presentations. A sum of money was made available from a small grant during the first year for the purpose of increasing the media center facilities of the school. Plans were drawn up and approved and Plate 9-5 shows the results. Stacks and carrels were built, more materials were purchased and the two rooms, with the accordion wall removed, became an outstanding example of a media center, office and all, for under $2000. Presently the school has approximately 550 students and boasts the following materials:

Books	8000	
Magazines	46	titles
Pamphlets	2000	under numerous headings
Transparencies	425	
Filmstrips	1203	
Paperbacks	448	

    The state of New York has several educational agencies which assist school districts in many ways. One of these is BOCES (Board of Cooperative Educational Services). As one of its many services, BOCES publishes much material concerning the uses of media to

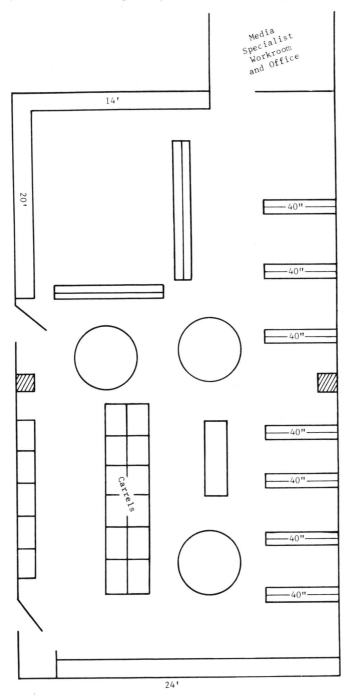

Plate 9-5

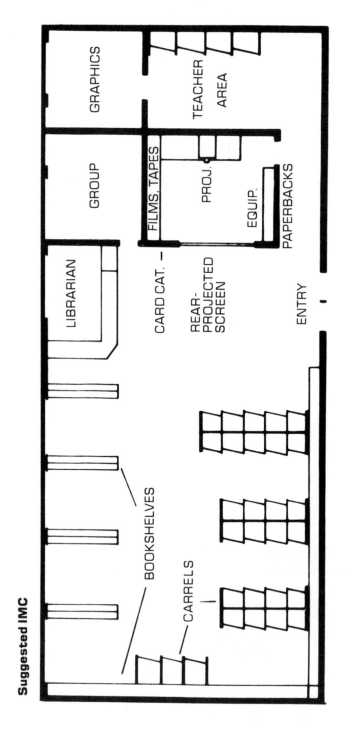

Plate 9-6

Suggested Changes in School

Present Library

Connecting Classroom

enhance educational programs. Plate 9-6 demonstrates another method of connecting two rooms to enlarge and enhance the present library into an instructional media center. One of the highlights of this new expanded room is its projection room. This would contain all the films and tapes and projection equipment for the center. Children could watch a film or other visual presentation by sitting in front of the rear projection screen. There is also a teacher preparation room as well as a room for the preparation of graphics. Carrels provide for 29 children and four teachers.

Plate 9-7 is the presentation of a plan involving the use of two relocatable classroom modules. The cost of these units is much less than the cost of adding on rooms to the school. This material (in expanded form) is contained in *Using Instructional Media Effectively* by Jack Tanzman and Kenneth J. Dunn, (Parker Publishing Company, 1971.)

REDESIGN USING AN ENTIRE FLOOR

If the media center can be centrally located, it is possible to provide additional room by the use of corridor space. Since many school buildings are modeled on the single corridor with classrooms on both sides, let's try to adapt one of them to meet the expanding needs of the learner as they can be met by a well-placed media center. We start by removing the walls from the corridors and from between the classrooms. Of course, we would leave those girders and portions of walls necessary to support the ceiling, the air ducts, and/or the electrical conduits. The resulting structure should look like a very large room with girders placed strategically as the original architect determined they should be. What we have essentially is an open-space school. The center of the structure is now the media center, and it is surrounded by instructional areas which can be made flexible by the addition of folding or accordion walls and doors. There are various possibilities, all of which are more or less expensive.

Plates 9-8, 9-9, and 9-10[1] show how intelligent remodeling of an old school can actually change the entire educational program and enhance the environment to an extent impossible to imagine under the limitations of the old design. These plates come from one of the many booklets distributed by the New Life for Old Schools Project

---

1. These three Plates are printed by permission of Educational Facilities Laboratories, Inc., 477 Madison Avenue, New York, N. Y. 10022.

Alternate Proposal • Where space is at a premium, as it is in many elementary schools, the "blueprint for action" includes alternate suggestions. Two relocatable classroom modules could be combined to form a single unit that will house both library and media facilities, providing additional space within the school (possibly where the library is located) and a complete media center that is easily accessible to pupils and staff.

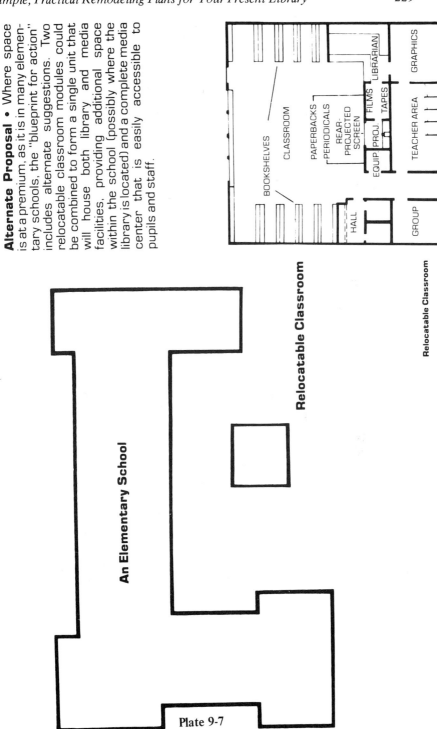

An Elementary School

Relocatable Classroom

Relocatable Classroom

BOOKSHELVES

CLASSROOM

PAPERBACKS

PERIODICALS

REAR-PROJECTED SCREEN

EQUIP. PROJ.

FILMS

TAPES

LIBRARIAN

GRAPHICS

TEACHER AREA

HALL

GROUP

Plate 9-7

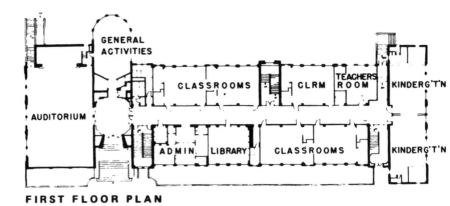

FIRST FLOOR PLAN

GENERAL ACTIVITIES

CLASSROOMS

CLRM

TEACHERS ROOM

KINDERG'T'N

AUDITORIUM

ADMIN.   LIBRARY   CLASSROOMS

KINDERG'T'N

SHELTER

CHILD CARE

CAFETERIA

GIRLS   BOYS

BOILER ROOM

KITCHEN

STORAGE

UNEXCAVATED

GROUND FLOOR PLAN

EXISTING FLOOR PLANS--JOHN MUIR
ELEMENTARY SCHOOL

Plate 9-8

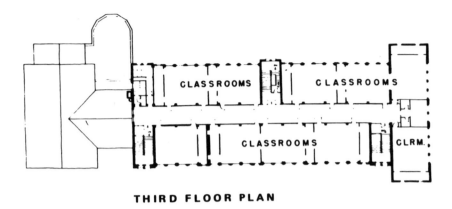

THIRD FLOOR PLAN

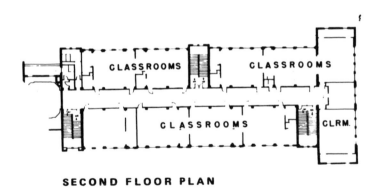

SECOND FLOOR PLAN

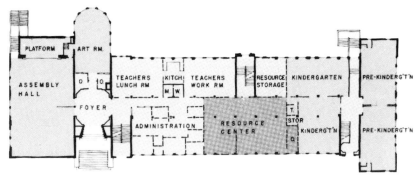

PROPOSED FIRST FLOOR PLAN

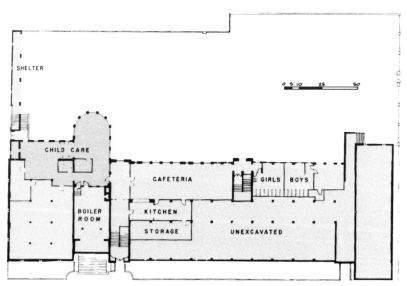

PROPOSED GROUND FLOOR PLAN

JOHN MUIR ELEMENTARY SCHOOL

Plate 9-9

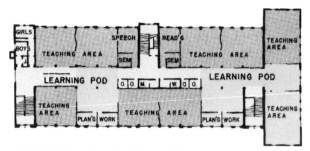

PROPOSED THIRD FLOOR PLAN

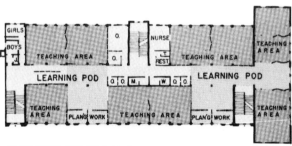

PROPOSED SECOND FLOOR PLAN

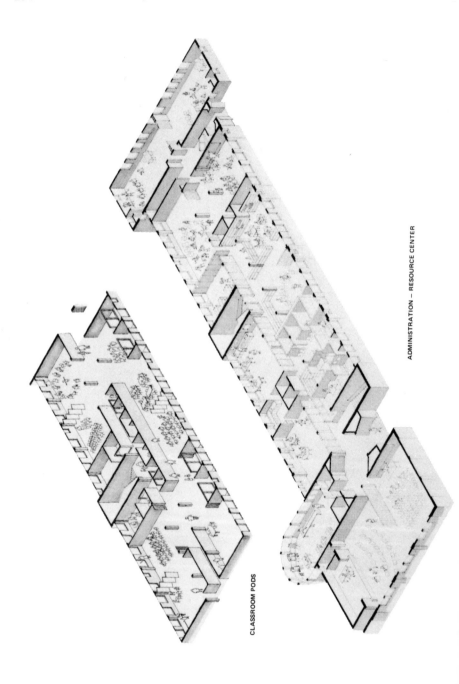

ADMINISTRATION – RESOURCE CENTER

CLASSROOM PODS

Plate 9-10

which is based in Chicago. The school referred to is the John Muir Elementary School in San Francisco. Pay special attention to the old first-floor plan on Plate 9-8 as compared to the proposed first-floor plan on plate 9-9. Then look carefully at the expanded first-floor administration-Resource Center on Plate 9-10 together with the classrooms on the second and third floor of the building. The complete remodeling of the John Muir School ran to over $900,000 but a new building of the same design would have cost close to $2,000,000. The construction costs of most new schools run as high as $30.00 per square foot.

A NOVEL PLAN FOR REDESIGNING A MEDIA CENTER FOR A TWO-STORY SCHOOL

Where there is some money available, a centrally located two-story media center could be designed which would serve the needs of primary and intermediate school children. The first floor could be connected to the second floor of the media center by the construction of circular stairwells. We would place all the picture books and fiction books and stacks on the second floor with areas for group story telling and lounge areas (armchairs, and couches, and lamps) for browsing, reading, and/or peer discussion. The media aide would have his desk here and he would also man a counter for book checkout. The first floor would be the area for concentration on reference material and media. All nonfiction stacks would be kept here. Also located in various areas would be study carrels (wet and dry), a rear projection screen and large-group viewing area, and teacher preparation areas. The media specialist should circulate through this floor using his special knowledge to direct children and teachers to the many varieties of material appropriate to their needs. His office and workroom would also be located on the first floor.

We have offered the preceding designs and design ideas for your consideration and use. You can probably come up with many more that would suit the needs of your schools. We hope you do.

There are many organizations which can help you with ideas to make a successful media center in your building. They are:

Educational Facilities Laboratory (EFL)
447 Madison Avenue, New York, N.Y. 10022
New Life for Old Schools Project
20 North Wacker Drive, Suite 1734, Chicago, Illinois 60606

10

Designing a Media Center
in a New School

A modern public library building represents much in concept and design that we would suggest for inclusion in any new school media center: shelves are set up as stacks; areas are set aside for casual browsing, book reading, newspaper scanning, magazine viewing; there are usually small rooms for listening; one can find a reproducing machine for copying text or pictures; a microfilm file and viewer are generally available; areas with tables and chairs are located for general studying; there are at least one or two sections with lamps, chairs, and sofas where casual reading or small group discussions can take place. Located in various places adjacent to the library are offices which are used for filing, for workshops, and for the production of materials. About the only things lacking are projection rooms and equipment for this kind of viewing, and wet carrels; although there may be one or two libraries which are advanced enough to provide these services to the public.

MODERN PUBLIC LIBRARY AS HEART OF NEW SCHOOL

If we were to take this modern public library building and add a shell around and above it where children could meet, and then staff this shell with instructional personnel and aides, design flexible partitions, add study carrels (wet and dry), equip this additional space with books and supplies, and install lighting with variable controls, we should then have created a very useful educational structure which would serve the needs of a much larger community than that for which it was originally designed. We will deal with many outstanding designs later in this chapter, but we must first discuss the rationale for designing new educational structures for media.

OPEN SPACE PRECEDENT IN ONE-ROOM SCHOOLHOUSE

Many new school designs place their learning areas in large, open areas called clusters, pods, or just open space. These spaces, with the addition of various kinds of furniture and partition devices, can be used to provide many kinds of instructional arrangements including diverse grouping patterns to allow for individual instruction or multi-age groupings. If this sounds familiar—it is! The old, one-room schoolhouse is actually the prototype of the open space concept. There were various age and intellectual disparities among the many pupils in that structure; the teacher, however, was expected to reach the needs of each of these students. The pendulum has swung many times since, but each new swing carried with it the weight of additional evidence about the learning process and the teaching process, about the accumulation of facts and the seeking after knowledge, about the copious accretion of materials and devices which now make this seeking so fruitful. We have also learned something about freedom and choice, so we must include this in our planning for the future.

SELF-CONTAINED CLASSROOM ANTECEDENTS

When larger school buildings were finally built they reflected the social needs of the builders: school was a place to hold children. Although learning did take place, it did so under some rather mean conditions. Poor lighting, poor heating, and poor insulation were only a few of the environmental conditions with which students and teachers had to cope. Worse than these was the rigidity of the classroom. Desks were fastened to the floor and the appearance was that children were fastened to the desks. All children were expected to participate in the same lesson at the same time regardless of ability or preparedness. Finally, each classroom was sealed off from its neighbor by thick walls and doors. Thus, the self-contained classroom had come into its own with little of the democracy of the one-room schoolhouse; unfortunately it still holds its own in too many places.

DESIGN SCHOOLS FOR CHILDREN AND FLEXIBILITY

James Grand, former principal of the Lewis Sands School in Chagrin Falls, Ohio, offers the following on the self-contained classroom: "It's time we built buildings that take into account human nature. For a long time schools have been built to please board members or architects, not children. The self-contained classroom is unreal. It is the only place in our whole society where one person has supreme authority over 30 other people— children—for most of their waking hours" (*Schools Without Walls;* Educational Facilities Laboratory, 1968; pp. 53-54).

Not only was the old school undemocratic in concept, its architecture which was often ugly to look at and be in offered other problems, economic ones. In the *Educational Equipment and Materials'* Seminar issue of 1968, Dr. Harold Gores talked about this: "The problem with our old schools is that they haven't been good places for people, and so, therefore, you are stuck with the school, and it is the wrong place, and finally you abandon it.

"The old school is no good," he continues. "It's a bad deal for the private sector to take a(n) . . . obsolete building fit only for children to be held in. The thing is no good for anybody. The kind of industry that would move into the typical abandoned New York City schoolhouse would find that its image was damaged. They wouldn't put their name over the door" (p. 43).

John L. Reid, F.A.I.A., an architect from San Francisco participating in the same seminar, added the following: "The best way to solve the problem of the obsolete and unusable school building is to design today's schools with the maximum of flexibility. Many of the schools that are being built today are not flexible enough" (p. 44).

We concur with this. Philosophically it is easier to bring about instructional change and the introduction of new concepts in learning and teaching in a new school. Flexibility can be designed in terms of the use of space, and there is no building impediment to innovation. There is always enough electrical power available— an absolute must in designing schools for media. Most importantly, the media center can be built as a central or core area.

HIGHLIGHTS OF SCHOOLS USING MEDIA

Other ideas for your consideration can be found in *Highlights of Schools Using Educational Media* (Department of Audio Visual

Instruction, NEA; March 1969): "Survey teams also found that individual schools having IMC's (Instructional Materials Centers) were those which were designed, built, and equipped for the purpose of an optimum use of media. The newest of such schools are air-conditioned, have no windows, and are built 'in the round', with the carpeted IMC at the heart of the building, and with classrooms built as pods around this center. In many of these new schools, classrooms have movable walls to permit team teaching of large and small groups, and to promote individualized instruction—part of it through locally produced programed instruction. Most of these facilities have study carrels equipped with electrical outlets for self-instruction through the use of remote access to both audio and visual instructional material. . . . The evidence appears to be conclusive that newer construction facilitates the use of new techniques" (pp. 302-3).

PROBLEMS IN DESIGNING AND BUILDING NEW SCHOOLS

Taking everything into consideration, the new school building represents a considerable investment on the part of the taxpayers. It must be carefully and thoughtfully planned. Too many schools have been built to satisfy the severe economics of the community as interpreted by the laymen on the board of education. These plants are then thrown to the resources of the professional educators and administrators who promptly uncover the major educational defects and limitations of the structure, and who are told, just as promptly, that they should be thankful for the new and should be prepared to show the community the results the board anticipates from the new edifice. To avoid this kind of well meaning ignorance, it has been suggested that a school be built three times, once by the educators, once by the architects, and once by the builders. This necessary cooperation and consultation can only result in the kinds of structures that continue to serve the needs of a community for many, many years. Several of the outstanding school designs which will be described in the next few pages were a result of just the kind of consultation suggested above. Some had been in the planning for several years.

IDEAS TO CONSIDER FOR MEDIA-DESIGNED SCHOOLS

There are several ideas we feel you should keep in mind when you think about designing a new school for media. The media center should be the heart of your plan. Every student should have access to its resources several times a day. The learning areas should be completely flexible. By this we mean having the ability to arrange partitions to make large spaces, small spaces, and closed spaces, if these are desirable. Lighting should be considered to provide a variety of levels for each area. With variable controls any one area could be used for a motion picture showing at one time, a science lab at another time, an art room at another, and so on. Movable partitions should be so constructed that they provide a sound barrier when they are used to close off an area. Floors should be carpeted because carpeting is both economical and soft underfoot, as well as being easy to maintain. An additional advantage is the esthetic one of a quiet interior due to the sound-absorbing propensities of quality carpet. If there are windows, these should be so constructed that complete closure devices can keep out all external light and glare during film presentations. Because media require so much ancillary equipment which uses electricity, there should be sufficient outlets and power sources to provide this power to any and all parts of the structure. Air conditioning used to be considered a frill for educational plants in most parts of the country. In many places it still is. After all, the reasoning goes, kids don't need air conditioning; just open the windows. This doesn't work too well when there is no wind, of course. Nor does it improve concentration when the temperature reaches above 90 degrees. It is quite possible that many children waste two months every year under sweltering, highly distracting conditions. Since most new industrial plants include air conditioning in their planning, it is conceivable that new educational plants should include it as well. In any case, teacher groups will probably be asking for air conditioning as a condition of employment.

We will now present floorplans, photos, and descriptions of several elementary and middle school buildings from different parts of the United States. These structures were erected during 1969 and 1970. They were featured at the annual Exhibition of School Architecture held at the American Association of School Administrators' annual convention in Atlantic City, New Jersey.

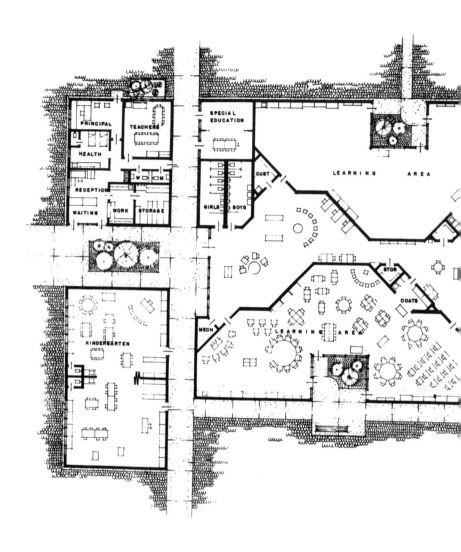

Plate 10-1

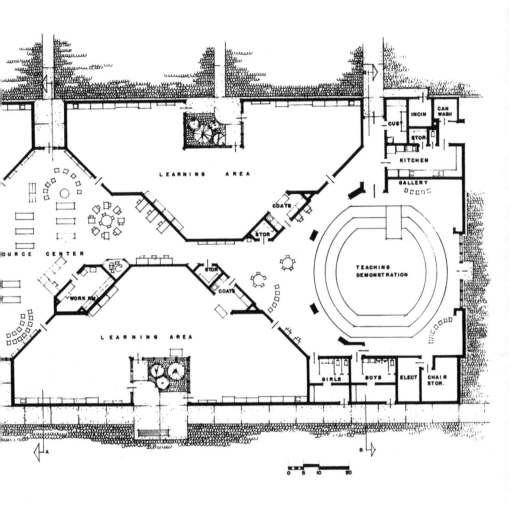

DAFFODIL VALLEY ELEMENTARY SCHOOL, SUMNER, WASH-
INGTON

Donald F. Burr & Associates, Architects

Plate 10-1: Floorplan

The media center (called the resource center) becomes the literal
heart of the school as you can see in this drawing. Notice how the
media center acts as the corridor and passageway from each learning
area to the teacher demonstration area at the right. This satisfies our
requirements for each student having ready access to the media
center several times daily. The media center in this school has been
designed as an integral part of the learning environment.

Plate 10-2:   Photo of Resource Center
              Daffodil Valley Elementary School
              Photographer: Jini Dellaccio

In this photo are seen the great variety of materials with which the

Plate 10-2

resource center supports the educational program: artwork, graphics, programmed materials, tapes, records, films, and a great abundance and variety of books to which both students and teachers have easy access, and which are highly visible.

BRYANT WOODS ELEMENTARY SCHOOL, HOWARD COUNTY, MARYLAND

McLeod, Ferrara & Ensign, Architects

Plate 10-3: Floorplan

This 600-pupil school has the media center as the heart of its structure. There is easy access from the classroom cluster areas to the center. Notice the many desirable features: small-group instructional areas, teacher's workroom, the visual and audio workroom, the special purpose classroom. The various clusters are open space and provide for a variety of grouping arrangements.

APOLLO ELEMENTARY SCHOOL, MILFORD, MICHIGAN

Richard Prince & Associates, Architects

Plate 10-4: Floorplan

This elementary school has been designed for the use of 600 children from kindergarten to sixth grade. Unlike the Bryant Woods design, the kindergarten and first grade units are separated from the media center. The second through sixth grade units, however, are wrapped around it. Notice the teacher workrooms and the A-V storage room adjacent to the center.

Plate 10-5: Photo of Instructional Materials (Media Center)
        Apollo Elementary School
        Photographer: Douglas Lyttle

Carpeting provides a soft, sound-absorbing floor for the center. The center is equipped with portable carts which bring material to the students. Individual and group areas add dimension to the use of this center.

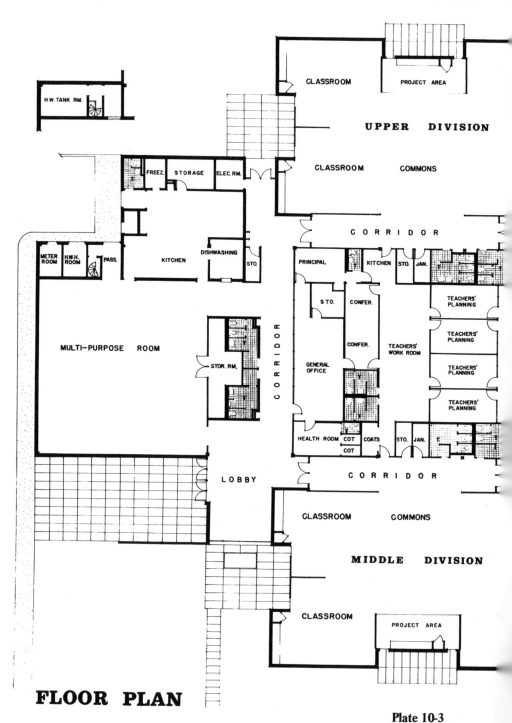

FLOOR PLAN

Plate 10-3

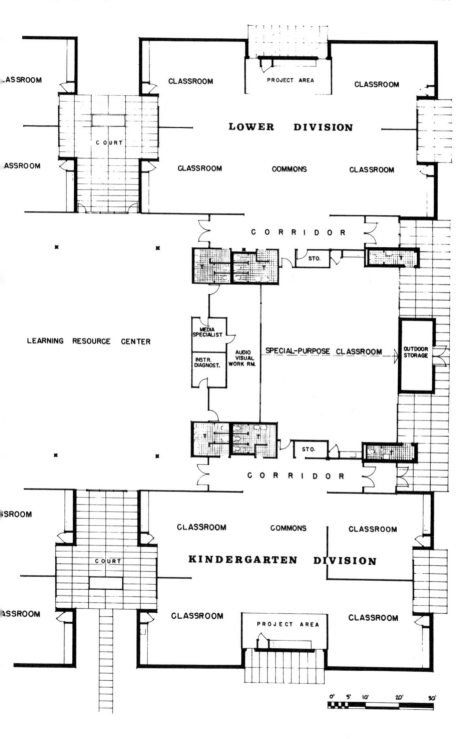

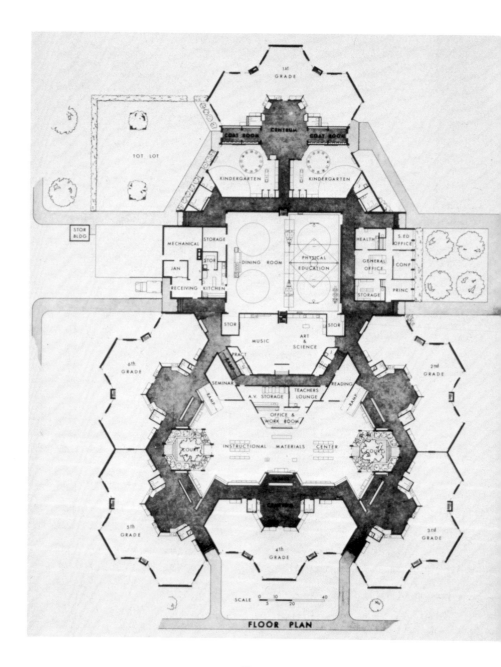

Plate 10-4

Plate 10-5

LEO J. MUIR ELEMENTARY SCHOOL, BOUNTIFUL, UTAH
Harold K. Beecher & Associates, Architects

Plate 10-6: Two level floorplan

Here again, the kindergarten and first grade sections are separated from the rest of the school. They are on a different level. The five group learning centers from grades two through six are adjacent to and become part of the instructional materials center.

PATAPSCO MIDDLE SCHOOL, HOWARD COUNTY, MARYLAND
Johannes and Murray & Associates, Architects

Plate 10-7: Floorplan

Although this school was designed to meet the needs of sixth to eighth grade students, many elements in its open space design must be considered as applicable to the planning of any new school, whatever level, for the use of media. Again, the core of the plan is

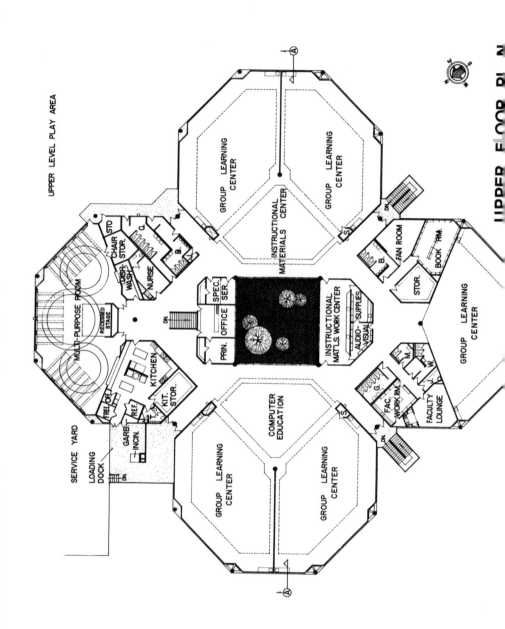

Plate 10-6

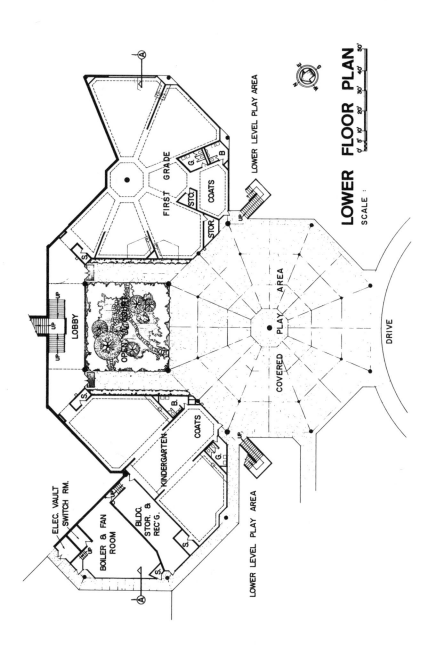

LOWER FLOOR PLAN

SCALE :

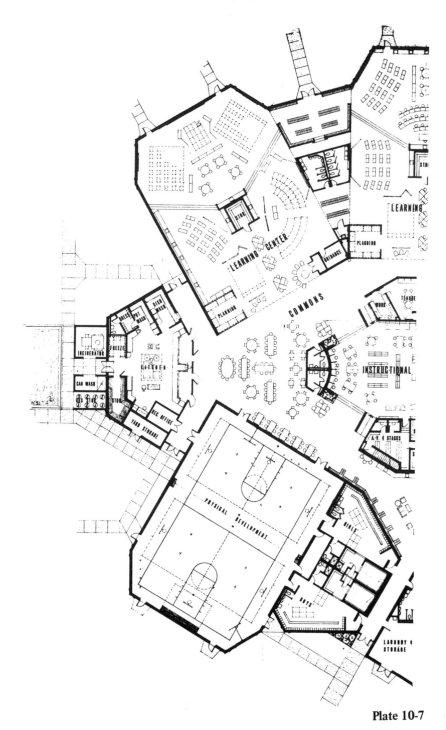

Plate 10-7

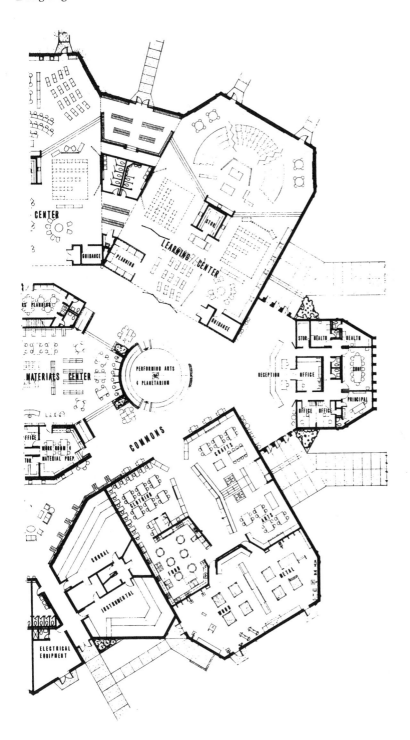

the instructional materials (media) center and teacher planning center, and planetarium-performing arts area. Notice the three convertible pods or learning centers for academic activities. These learning centers have open instructional areas and spaces which can be arranged in any number of ways, as well as work areas which are four steps below the learning area. The convertible areas in this plan are designed to facilitate changing teaching methods, changing programs, and changing enrollments. The school is also equipped with light dimmers, closed circuit T.V., and electronic teaching equipment.

WALNUT HILLS ELEMENTARY SCHOOL, ARAPAHOE COUNTY, COLORADO

William C. Haldeman, Architect

Plate 10-8: Floorplan

The school was planned with flexible, open instructional areas and provisions made for future changes in the educational program, including a return to conventional classroom space if desired. The whole school was designed to act as a library or educational materials center. The area at the center of the unit at right is the library-commons area, including instructional media of all kinds, study carrels, and adjoining teacher planning areas. The four large instructional areas (one of which is a future addition) are grouped around the library. The school-community library is located at the center, adjacent to the main entry, with a multi-purpose room at the far left.

SOUTHLAWN MIDDLE SCHOOL, ROCKVILLE, MARYLAND

Stanley H. Arthur, Architect

Plate 10-9: Floorplan

The instructional materials center, located at the core of the classroom building, has been planned for flexible arrangement of spaces and furnishings to meet changing functions and to make multiple use of this space. Individual study and conference areas, seminar rooms, and resource areas are located nearby.

We hope that these glimpses of new schools and their media centers have provided you with insights into some design considerations which may help you plan better for educating students in your district. The following references were most enlightening to us and may provide you with explicit information for designing new buildings for the use of media:

Educational Facilities with New Media
Department of Audiovisual Instruction,
National Education Association
  in collaboration with
Center for Architectural Research,
Rensselaer Polytechnic Institute

Highlights of Schools Using Educational Media
Department of Audiovisual Instruction,
National Education Association

School Buildings 1969 Filmstrip and Discussion Manual,*
School Buildings 1970 Filmstrip and Discussion Manual
American Association of School Administrators, with
  assistance from the Division of Facilities Development
  of the U.S. Office of Education
National Education Association,
Washington, D.C.

---

*Note: School Buildings, Filmstrips and Discussion Manuals are an annual series.

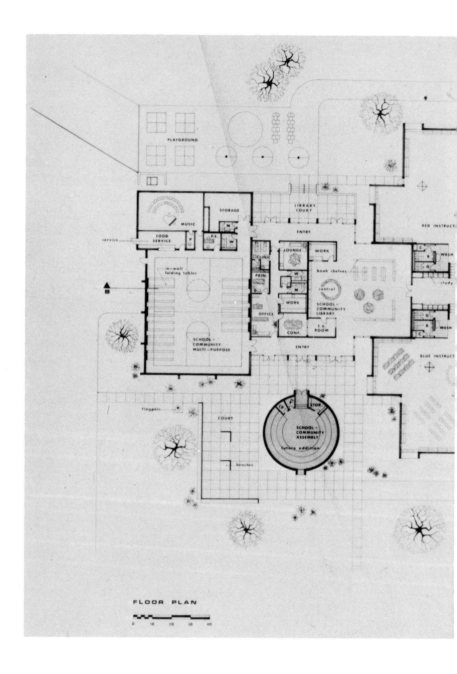

Plate 10-8

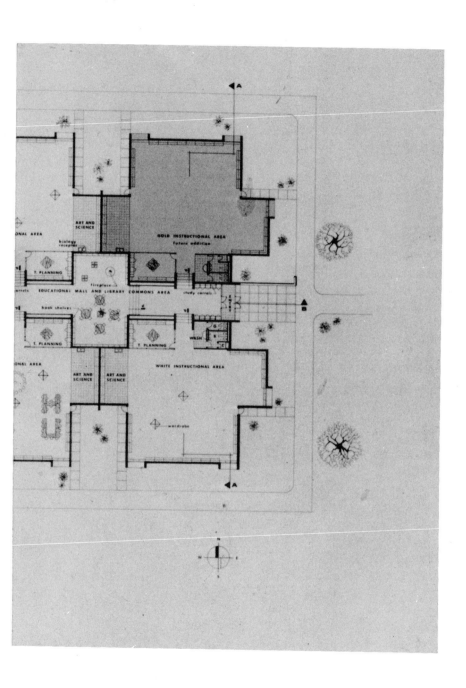

Plate 10-9

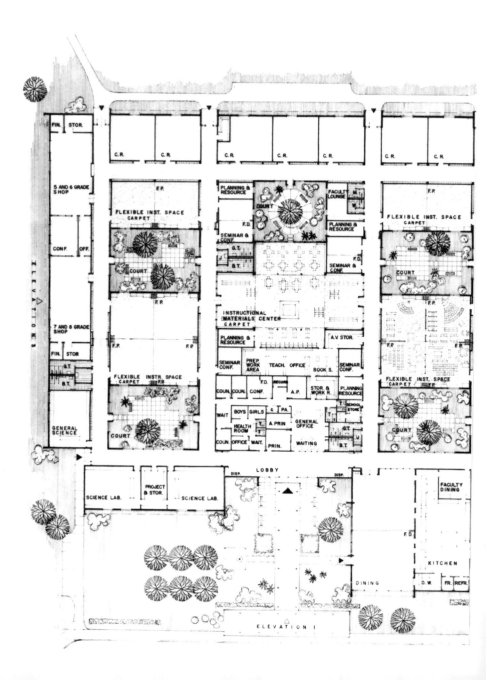

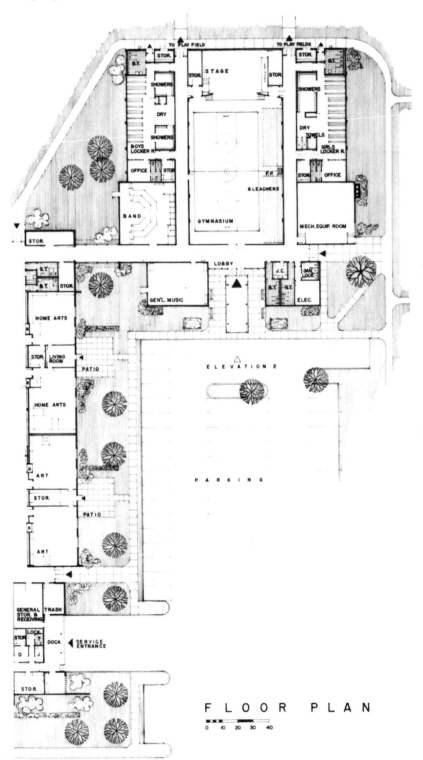

F L O O R   P L A N

0   10   20   30   40

APPENDIX

ANSWERS TO GAMES AND PUZZLES

VOCABULARY PUZZLE

1. periodical
2. reference (spelled backwards)
3. dictionary
4. pamphlets; information file
5. fiction
6. picture file
7. biography
8. booktruck
9. studyprint and poster case
10. card catalog
11. carrel
12. faculty
13. charging desk; card sorter
14. nonfiction
15. disc

FIND THE BIRDIE

k 1. Duckling
h 2. Owls
f 3. Goose
c 4. Owls
d 5. Heron
k 6. Swans
e 7. Crane
a 8. Crow
g 9. Penguins
l 10. Crow

b 11. Rooster
j 12. Robin
i 13. Canary

SOME LIKE IT HOT, SOME LIKE IT COLD

(C) Winter *danger*
(F) *The* summer *I was lost*
(H) *Wild*fire
(B) *The long* winter
(M) *The very* hot *water bottle*
(G) Burning *mountain*
(J) *When the* ice *came*
(E) *Danger* iceberg *ahead!*
(K) Flaming *arrows*
(D) *Thin* ice
(L) *The* summer snow *man*
(A) *The* snow *queen*
(I) Snow *dog*

ANIMAL TRAFFIC

Ralph—motorcycle
Mr. Toad—car or boat
Carbonel—broom
Chester—picnic basket
Curious George—boat
Katy—apron pocket
Ping—sampan
Anatole—bicycle
Babar and Celeste—balloon
Flyball—spaceship
Stuart Little—canoe, car, sailboat, and bird.

TOGETHERNESS

Wendy Darling—Peter Pan
Latsi—Dangerous Journey
Zephir—Babar and His Children
Mowgli—Jungle Books
Commander Crackpot—Chitty Chitty Bang Bang

Jancsi—The Good Master
Charlie Bucket—Charlie and the Chocolate Factory
Nate Twitchell—The Wonderful Egg
Amy March—Little Women
Almanzo—Farmer Boy
Paddington—A Bear Named Paddington
Johnny Tremain—Johnny Tremain
Milo—Phantom Tollbooth

WHO IS WHO IN THIS ZOO?

A. (10,h)
B. (6,d)
C. (5,a)
D. (3,b)
E. (2,j)
F. (11,k)
G. (12,i)
H. (4,f)
I. (8,e)
J. (9,g)
K. (7,b)
L. (1,c)

NAME CALLING

The Prince and the Pauper—Edmund Tudor
The Little Princess—Sara Crewe
Weaver of Dreams—Charlotte Brontë
The Good Master—Marton Nagy
Fire Hunter—Hawk
Plain Girl—Esther Lapp
The youngest of Little Women—Beth March
Wilderness Bride—Corey Tremaine
The Pigman—Mr. Pignati
The Hobbit—Bilbo Baggins
Farmer Boy—Almanzo Wilder
The Little Lame Prince—Prince Dolor
My Father's Dragon—Elmer Elevator

STRANGE CRITTERS

J. – H. C. Andersen
E. – Dr. Seuss
L. – Finian's daughter
M. – Juno
B. – Alice
H. – Jonathan Swift
I. – Dr. Dolittle
K. – Reynard the Fox
D. – C. S. Lewis
G. – Tolkien
N. – Lewis Carroll
F. – Barnstable children
A. – Edward Lear
C. – White witch

IT'S A DOG'S LIFE

Dorothy–Toto
David–Rinty
Henry–Ribsy
Duke–Otto
John Thornton–Buck
Fred–Mike
Travis–Old Yeller
Danny–Big Red
Jase–Sputters
The Darlings–Nana
Madeline–Genevieve
Peter–Willie
Miss Marvelous–Pumpkin, Ginger and Spice

INDEX HUNT

<u>3</u>   Q. What animal can break off its tail and grow a new one?
       A. A lizard

<u>5</u>   Q. Why were our great-great-great-grandmothers afraid to eat
       tomatoes?
       A. In the old days tomatoes were thought to be poisonous

because they belong to the same family as the deadly night-shade.

3   Q. Does handling toads cause warts?
     A. No, that is a superstition.

2   Q. How long does a box turtle live?
     A. 70-80 years

2   Q. Are vitamins food?
     A. No

4   Q. Where is the world's largest reflecting telescope?
     A. Mount Palomar, California

1   Q. Which continent is the home of the tiger?
     A. Asia

4   Q. How do ants defend themselves?
     A. By biting, stinging, spitting out a disagreeable liquid and playing dead

3   Q. Which bird has the greatest wingspread?
     A. The wandering albatross: 11 feet from tip to tip

3   Q. In which states is Arbor Day celebrated in winter?
     A. In Southern states like Louisiana, Arkansas, Texas

5   Q. At what time of day did the ancient Greeks give theatrical performances?
     A. During the daytime

5   Q. What president of the United States later became Chief Justice of the Supreme Court?
     A. William Howard Taft

4   Q. Why do today's soldiers wear dull colored uniforms?
     A. For camouflage

5   Q. Why do leaves change color in the fall?
     A. In the fall a layer of cells forms at the base of the leaves, which does not let chlorophyll pass through. The green in the leaves disappears and the other colors show up.

4   Q. Of which bridge in the U.S. is the main span 1212 feet long?
     A. The Tappan Zee Bridge over the Hudson, between Nyack and Tarrytown, N. Y.

3   Q. What is the name of the largest lake in the world?
     A. The Caspian Sea in Russia

4   Q. Which is the longest passenger railroad tunnel in the world?

A. The Simplon Tunnel in Switzerland

5   Q. Who was Vice-President when Lincoln was President?
    A. Hannibal Hamlin and Andrew Johnson

3   Q. When did the Saint Louis Cardinals last win the World Series?
    A. In 1967

4   Q. What insects keep slaves?
    A. Ants

3   Q. What do parasol ants grow for food?
    A. A fungus grown on leaves they have chewed up

2   Q. Which is colder, the Arctic or the Antarctic?
    A. The Antarctic

1   Q. What is the "Christ of the Andes"?
    A. A statue in the Andes Mountains on the border between Chile and Argentina

5   Q. What was the Gordian knot?
    A. A tight knot which was cut by Alexander the Great at Gordium.

2   Q. According to legend, how did King Arthur prove his right to the throne?
    A. By removing a sword from a stone, which no one else had been able to do

4   Q. Why were spiders (Arachnidae) named for a mythical girl?
    A. When Arachne claimed to be a better weaver than the goddess Athena she was punished for her arrogance and turned into a spider.

1   Q. Where does the bottle tree grow and why is it so called?
    A. In Australia; it is shaped like a bottle

3   Q. How does Los Angeles get its water supply?
    A. Through aqueducts from Owens Valley in the Sierra Nevada and the Colorado River

3   Q. Why is the Pacific Ocean bluer than the Atlantic?
    A. More plankton in the Atlantic screens its surface color

2   Q. How did Mark Twain get his name?
    A. He took this Mississippi term, meaning <u>two fathoms deep,</u> as his pen name.

1   Q. How can you tell Poison Ivy from Virginia Creeper?

A. Poison Ivy has three and Virginia Creeper has five leaves on a stem.

5   Q. How much water may a medium-sized apple tree soak up on one summer day?
A. 94 gallons

5   Q. What are the four differences between a plant and an animal?
A. Plants contain cellulose, chlorophyll; make their own food; and cannot move from place to place by themselves.

2   Q. How long is a newly hatched alligator?
A. About 8 inches

5   Q. Of what wood are baseball bats made?
A. White ash, cottonwood and sweetgum

1   Q. What is a sampler?
A. a piece of embroidery

4   Q. When and where was Arbor Day first celebrated?
A. April 10, 1872 in Nebraska

2   Q. What is a trundle bed? Find a picture.
A. A bed on wheels which is stored under another bed and which is rolled out when needed

4   Q. What animals live from 30-40 years?
A. bear, owl, eagle crane, hippopotamus

2   Q. What kind of food does an armadillo eat?
A. Ants

3   Q. What is another name for a carrier pigeon?
A. homing pigeon or homer

1   Q. Where did the tomato come from?
A. From South America

4   Q. Who discovered the X-ray?
A. Wilhelm Roentgen

5   Q. Find the name of a plant that eats insects.
A. Venus fly trap, pitcher plant or sundew

4   Q. If you like chocolate you should be grateful to the__Aztecs__
_____who first used it as a drink.

HISTORIC OPPONENTS

Hannibal—18
Lee—21
Custer—13
Santa Ana—2
Douglas—16
Cornwallis—11
Burgoyne—14
Caesar—1
Cortez—8
Pershing—15
Napoleon—6
Monitor—17
Hector—3
Cyrus the Great—22
Saladin—19
Gladstone—5
Nixon—12
Pizarro—20
Judas Maccabeus—10
Demosthenes—9
Capulets—4
Alexander Hamilton—7

NAME THEIR FAME CONTEST No. 3

Addams, Jane: social worker
Anderson, Marian: singer
Audubon, John: artist-naturalist
Bunche, Ralph: diplomat
Drew, Charles: blood researcher
Evers, Medgar: civil rights worker
Gershwin, George: composer
Harris, Patricia: ambassador
Hughes, Langston: poet
Marshall, Thurgood: Supreme Court Justice
Matisse, Henri: painter
Mayo (Brothers): doctors
Price, Leontyne: opera singer
Thurber, James: author, artist
Wilkins, Roy: NAACP president

A SPORTING CHANCE

7. wrestling
4. swimming
8. boxing
10. football
13. baseball
12. tennis—men's singles
3. figure skating
6. golf
2. channel swimming
1. tennis—women's singles
9. track
5. sharpshooting
11. mountaineering

LINCOLN CONTEST:

Grace Bedell from Westfield, N.Y.

WASHINGTON CONTEST:

Parson Mason Locke Weems, a bookseller and writer.

MONSTER GALLERY

i—The Cyclops, Polyphemus
f—Minotaur
j—Cerberus
a—Goliath
g—Geryon
h—Medusa
b—Merlin
k—Fafner
e—Grendel
d—Roc
c—Sphinx

THE MAGIC NUMBER 3

Flopsy, Mopsy and Cottontail
The 3 kittens
Abercrombie, Benjamin and Christopher
Owl, pussycat, piggywig
Butcher, baker, candlestick maker
The 3 bears
The 3 little pigs
The 3 billy goats Gruff
The 3 blind mice

WHERE ARE THE TITLES?

If I ran the zoo
A funny thing
Madeline
Oliver
Julius
Blueberries for Sal
Over in the meadow
One morning in Maine
Lentil
Madeline
Friendly animals
Millions of cats
Angus and the ducks
Julius
Madeline
The biggest bear
A tiger called Thomas
Ferdinand the bull
Oliver
Curious George
Put me in the zoo
The elephant who liked to
  smash small cars

Flying patchwork quilt
Animals from everywhere
Birthday party
Animal frolic
Pancakes for breakfast
Hundreds and hundreds of pancakes
The biggest bear
Three little pigs
The three billy goats Gruff
Peter Rabbit
Harry the dirty dog
Timothy Turtle
The rooster crows
Ape in a cape
My father's dragon
Stone soup
Sugarplum
Do you know what I'll do?
Come and have fun
Oliver
Hurry, hurry
Down, down the mountain
Bedtime for Frances

FIND YOUR HIDDEN BOOKWEEK
READING LIST

I, Juan de Pareja
The swing in the summer house
My side of the mountain
Alvin's secret code
Storm from the West
Nightbirds on Nantucket
Flaming arrows
Shadow of a bull
Winter danger
Ready or not
Trail through danger
The Hobbit
Harriet the spy
Daughter of the mountains
Dangerous journey
Henry Reed, Inc.
A dog on Barkham Street
Seventeenth Street Gang
Charlie and the chocolate factory
The whirling shapes
No boats on Bannermere

The big wave
By secret railway
Family grandstand
Silence over Dunkerque
Lotte's locket
The empty schoolhouse
A family of foxes
Captains courageous
Landslide!
The summer I was lost
Five boys in a cave
The undergrounders
The night of the wall
. . .And now Miguel
The survivor
The loner
Banner in the sky
The winged watchman
An adventure in Bangkok
A wonderful terrible time

WINTER HOLIDAY QUIZ (primary)

1. Florida, Louisiana, Mississippi
2. Drink or dessert often served at holiday time
3. A top, used to play Hanukkah game
4. No
5. 8 plus 1 to light the others
6. Mexican Christmas procession, reenacting Joseph's and Mary's search for shelter, by going from house to house
7. Kris Kringle
8. Pere Noël
9. Yul Tomten
10. Hot chocolate; carrots, hay and water
11. Pinata
12. Judea or Palestine
13. A food trough or bin
14. Yes

WINTER HOLIDAY QUIZ (intermediate)

1. Helleborus niger
2. Only the female tree does
3. 12 days, from Christmas to Epiphany
4. N for Nes; G for Gadol; H for Hayah; S for Sham. Nes Gadol Hayah Sham means: A great miracle happened here.
5. Diseases of the lungs and chest, (formerly tuberculosis)
6. Potato pancakes (latkes)
7. Scandinavian countries
8. Mexico. . .the three kings
   Japan. . .Hoteiosho
   China. . .Lan Khoong-Khoong
   Denmark. . .Nisse
   Holland. . .Saint Nicholas (Sinterklaas)
   Germany. . .Christ child
9. The Maccabees
10. He had 2 faces, looking backward and forward at the same time and was the god of the beginning of things
11. To greet the New Year
12. A jar of oil with a one-day supply miraculously lasted for the eight days needed to reconsecrate the temple
13. To drink a toast
14. Antiochus Epiphanes

BEASTLY SYNONYMS

imitate—ape
dismay—cow
carry—bear
harass—hound
scold—nag
devour—swallow
joke—kid
find fault—carp
guide—steer
eat greedily—wolf
close tightly—seal
trail persistently—dog
take more than
    one's share—hog
fool around—horse around
press or force into place—ram
grouch—crab

VOWEL LANGUAGE

1. kraal	14. fiord
2. aerial	15. triumph
3. pail	16. soar
4. chaos	17. poem
5. gauche	18. void
6. lead	19. drool
7. leek	20. pouch
8. weight	21. safeguard
9. George	22. overdue
10. reunion	23. build
11. myriad	24. quotation
12. fierce	25. vacuum
13. skiing	

WORD OF THE MONTH

*Jan*itor
Li*feb*lood

*Mar*chpane
*Cap*rice
Dis*may*ed
In*jun*
*Jul*ep
*A*u*ger
*Sept*et
Pro*ct*or
Re*no*vate
In*dec*orous

PUT IN YOUR MONEY'S WORTH

Quick*silver*
De*note*
*Grand*iose
*Quarter*back
Inde*cent*
Pumper*nickel*
Con*fine*
*Dime*nsion
*Change*able
*Bond*age
Shoe*bill*
*Coin*cide
*Dough*ty
*Buck*le
*Cash*ew

FOR THE BIRDS

1. duck
2. lark
3. hawk
4. crow
5. crane
6. quail
7. grouse
8. parrot
9. swallow
10. flicker

11. cock
12. dove
13. snipe

WHAT DO WE MEAN AND WHERE DID WE BORROW?

Above board—honest—card playing
To bark up the wrong tree—to be wrong—hunting
You're on the beam—on the right course—flying
A baker's dozen—13 for 12—baking trade
Eating crow—to be made to do something unpleasant—War of 1812
On the nose—on time—broadcasting
Behind the eight ball—in a dangerous position—pool
It isn't cricket—not according to the rules—cricket

THREE IS NOT A CROWD HERE!

Melchior, Caspar, Balthasar
Tisiphone, Alecto, Megalia
Reading, writing, 'rithmetic
Shadrach, Meshach, Abednego
Clotho, Lachesis, Atropos
Charlotte, Emily, Anne
Serendip
Weird sisters
Ocypeta, Celeno, Aello
Athos, Porthos, Aramis

WHEN YOU THINK OF ONE
YOU THINK OF THE OTHER

Mutt—5
Hansel—8
Tinker Bell—6
Tweedledum—9
Jekyll—10
Romeo—11
Sullivan—12
Capt. John Smith—2
Peter Rabbit—3
Fiddle—14
Jack—4
Huck Finn—7
Tippecanoe—1
Frankie—13

IF YOU KNOW HOW TO BROWSE
YOU ARE NO SLOUCH

1. browsing
2. information
3. browse; faces
4. jacket
5. illustrator
6. print; small
7. letters; skinny
8. author
9. foreword; preface; introduction
10. author
11. nonfiction; index
12. browse

CLASSICAL CLASSIFIEDS

Help Wanted—14; 7.
Situations Wanted—15; 12; 9; 4.
Lost and Found—5; 3.
For Sale—13; 10; 1.
Equipment Wanted—11; 6.
Opportunities—8; 2.

WHO IS THE OTHER HALF?

Eve
Chloe
Psyche
Thisbe
Osiris
Baucis
Narcissus
Jonathan
Damon
Abel
Remus
Icarus
Pollux
Magog
Achilles

MYTH CROSSWORDS

Yama
Odin
Uranus
Ra
Leda
Icarus
Bacchus
Remus
Atlas
Rama
Ymir
Iphigenia
Quirinus

THE MESSY TOOLSHED

Gib Morgan—i
Mike Fink—e
Zeus—m
Paul Bunyan—j
Jim Bowie—b
Rumpelstiltskin—h
John Henry—a

Casey Jones—c
John Chapman—k
Cinderella—f
Pecos Bill—g
Davy Crockett—d
Neptune—l

SING-IN

1. The Erie Canal
2. Billy boy
3. 6 x 3
4. old horse-shay
5. Frankie
6. Captain Jinks of the
   horse marines
7. Annie Laurie
8. Ol' Paint
9. John Henry
10. Sir Patrick Spence
11. Clementine

MOTHER GOOSE HUNT

Peter White will never go right;
Would you know the reason
   why?
He follows his nose wherever he
   goes
And that stands all awry.

***

As I was going to sell my eggs,
I met a man with bandy legs,
Bandy legs and crooked toes,
I tript up his heels and he fell
   on his nose.

***

Little Robin Red Breast,
Sitting on a pole,
Niddle, Noddle,
Went his head,
And Poop went his hole.

There was an old woman
Lived under a hill,
And if she isn't gone,
She lives there still.

***

What's the news of the day,
Good neighbor, I pray?
They say the balloon
Is gone up to the moon!

***

Johnny Armstrong killed a calf,
Peter Henderson got half,
Willy Wilkinson got the head;
Ring the bell, the calf is dead.

***

Mirror, mirror tell me,
Am I pretty or plain?
Or am I downright ugly
And ugly to remain?

***

Hector Protector was dressed all
    in green,
Hector Protector was sent to
    the queen;
The queen did not like him,
No more did the king,
So Hector Protector was sent
    back again.

***

Lucy Locket lost her pocket,
Kitty Fisher found it;
Nothing in it, nothing in it
But the binding 'round it.

***

Barney Bodkin broke his nose,
Without feet we can't have toes;

Crazy folks are always mad,
Want of money makes me sad.

***

Alas, alas for Miss McKay,
Her knives and forks have run
   away;
And when the cups and spoons
   are going
She's sure there is no way of
   knowing.

***

Cackle, cackle, Mother Goose,
Have you any feathers loose?
Truly have I, pretty fellow,
Half enough to fill a pillow.
And here are quills, take one or
   ten,
And make from each, popgun
   or pen.

Index